Escape Rooms in Education

A practical guide

JULIA MORRIS

- p.31 idea

ISBN: 9798550449660

Contents

Part 1 Planning your escape room 6

Introduction 6

What is an escape room? 7

Why use it in school? 7

Can I use it for my class? 10

How do I plan the activity? 12

How do I come up with a story? 15

What is the difference between linear and non-linear setup? 18

What is the difference between digital, physical and mixed escape rooms? 21

What types of boxes and locks can I use? .. 27

How do I create digital rooms and locks? 32

What is good puzzle design? 43

What puzzles can I use? 47

How can I make it more immersive? 49

How do I organise the lesson and timing? .. 52

How do I give hints? 55

Can I see an example? 56

Part 2: Puzzles 58

How do I use the templates? 58

How do I make the code fit my lock? 59

Classic Elements 63

Hidden Objects 63
UV Light and Invisible Ink 67
QR Codes 70
Match up Puzzles 73
Code Wheel 73
Code String 76
Word Strips 78
Jigsaw Puzzles and Tarsias 80
Crosswords 83
Red Reveal 87
Transparency 90
Picture or Word Additions 92
Category Maze 94
Cards 97
Spot the Difference 100
Dot to Dot 102
Snotes 105
Colour Changer 108
Directional Maze 111
Number Changer 113
Text-based puzzles 115
Caesar Cipher 115
Cryptograms 118
Rebus 121

Substitution Ciphers 123
Acrostics and other fun with words 126
Scytale – wrapped up messages 129
Half text 131
Homophones and words within words....... 133
Logic Grid Puzzle...................................... 135
Word Clouds 139
Letter Maze.. 141
Cut Out 143
Scratch Card and Hidden Pictures 146
Text Wheel 149
Digital Puzzles 151
Learningapps, Bookwidgets and S'cape ... 151
360 Degree Views 155
Digital Variations on Multiple-choice 159
Example Escape Rooms 166
Example 1: Library induction..................... 166
Example 2: German numbers digital game 175
References 186
About the author 188

PART I PLANNING YOUR ESCAPE ROOM

Introduction

This practical guide to creating escape rooms is aimed at educators of all subjects and age groups. It will help you to feel confident in planning and conducting your own escape room lessons, either as a physical activity in the classroom or as a digital game, and your students will have a motivating and educational lesson, which they will remember for a long time to come.

The book has two parts: the first part explains what escape rooms are and why they are so popular in schools. It will provide an overview of the steps needed to plan your first breakout lesson and then look at each step in detail and provide advice and ideas. Part two is a collection of puzzle ideas that you can dip in and out of in any order to find inspiration for activities to use in your escape room. Each puzzle comes with instructions on how to create it, how students solve it and templates to help you create it quickly. I have also included some ideas how to use the puzzles in different subjects, and I hope that even if your subject is not included, reading them might spark an idea how to use it for your topic. If you would like to download an overview document that contains all web links included in this book, you can use this short link or QR code that can be found at the end of the book.

What is an escape room?

Escape rooms are a popular trend in the entertainment industry that first appeared at the beginning of the 2010s in Asia and can now be found all over the world. Escape rooms, also called escape games or breakout games, are team activities in which a group of people, typically friends or families, sometimes together with strangers, are locked into a room or a series of rooms and have to work collaboratively to find and solve clues hidden in the room in order to escape. The group has a time limit, usually an hour, and there are staff members available who will give an introduction, help with clues and stop the game when the time is up.

One of the most essential elements is the story or theme of the room, from "Find the secret spy in the World War II bunker" to "Get out of the Hogwarts classroom". For a successful escape game, the room needs to be decorated to allow for an immersive experience in which the players feel part of the story, and all puzzles need to link in with the theme. To allow for enjoyable team play, there need to be enough puzzles or hidden objects to keep everyone occupied. Ideally, different types of problem solvers will be able to find an activity to suit them: finding objects in hidden places, solving maths puzzles need, and overcoming physical challenges that require agility and speed.

Why use it in school?

The concept of the escape room is ideal for a unique, memorable lesson as they are fun experiences that require logical thinking, teamwork and subject knowledge. They take place within a limited time and location, which makes them perfect for a school setting where we must work within these constraints anyway.

Any subject or topic can be turned into an escape room, for any class size and any age group. They can be used to revise a topic or to introduce new material and research it with the help of computers or textbooks. The students will be so thrilled by the click of a lock opening after they applied a newly learned concept that it should stay in their memory much longer than if they just read it in a textbook.

Commercial escape rooms are extremely popular and can now be found in nearly all larger towns. You might find that a lot of older students have played one and they usually get very excited about the idea of playing in a lesson. Even if they have not heard of it before, the story and teamwork in an escape room lessons are very motivating. They will get everyone involved, even students that are not normally interested in the subject. The fact that the tasks are part of a story will drive students to solve all questions within the time limit. In an ideal case it can even show them how the subject matter can be applied in the real world: using maths to triangulate a point on a map, languages to decipher a letter written in French or chemistry to analyse the traces of a crime.

An added bonus with escape rooms is "the validation comes quickly and is integrated into the game"[1] as Robert and Sarah Ross point out in their book about educational breakout games. Every task is immediately rewarded by receiving a code or opening a lock, which

---

[1] Ross, Robert and Ross, Sarah (2020) *Inescapable Learning: Unlock the power of educational escape rooms,* Independently Published

keeps motivation high, and the feeling of success is increased by celebrating together with teammates.

Unlike the "escape the room" games that students might be playing on their phones, school escape rooms are designed as team tasks, even if you decide to create them in a virtual world with digital activities. Either the whole class or smaller teams have to work together and practise their communication skills to solve the tasks. Escape room lessons can be a good icebreaker and team-building exercise for a new group of people because they will have to work together to organise solving the tasks and they will get to know each other's strengths and weaknesses quickly. It can be a very valuable learning experience for the group to realise that when they get stuck, they can help each other with their individual strengths to overcome challenges.

Turing your room into a brain-teasing adventure is excellent training for independent, logic and strategic thinking. If the puzzles and tasks are varied enough, different types of students will have their opportunity to shine: some are better at putting together jigsaw puzzles, others might be able to think outside the box, and a third might be great at spotting hidden words in a jumbled text. I have been surprised in my classes that students, who are normally not a fan of my subject, suddenly work with enthusiasm and say they cannot possibly leave the lesson before they have found the solution to a tricky puzzle.

Every typical lesson in school has a set time limit, so it is surprising how much tension and excitement can be created by turning on a ticking clock and presenting the time limit as part of a story: "In one hour the hacker will release a virus into our network which will disable all student devices!"

Competition between teams and the promise of a prize are highly motivating and will make most classes work much faster and be more engaged in the tasks than the constant reminder that what they are learning will be useful for the next exam or "for life". Prizes can be given out for the fastest team or the whole group if everybody manages to escape, either in the form of "bragging rights" – having your victory photo taken and displayed in the school – or with actual prize objects like stickers, stationary or sweets.

It cannot be denied that escape room games do take more time and effort to prepare and set up than regular lessons. Still, the increase in motivation as well as the learning taking place, not only of subject matter but also of team working skills and logic, make them worth it. Once prepared, they can be used every year with a new generation of students and adapted for different topics as well as shared with colleagues. The advice and puzzle templates below aim to guide you step-by-step to make both the creation and the playing of your game an enjoyable process.

Can I use it for my class?

The concept of the escape game is a type of activity independent of content and can be adapted for any age group, subject and class size.

Players of any age can enjoy a breakout game. I have created an escape room for my son's seventh birthday party, and he enjoyed it just as much as the 18-year olds in my languages exam class. The success of the escape room industry shows that you are never too old to enjoy this type of game as millions of adults and families worldwide pay to be locked up to solve fiendish puzzles. Most of the puzzles in this book can be adapted to the ability of the students by using shorter text or pictures or by giving more direct instructions on how to solve them. A teaching assistant in my school built and ran an escape room with a group of students with special educational needs and they learned valuable organisational skills in planning the activity and manual skills in building mazes, turnable wheels and secret mirrors. Younger students will find more practical, hands-on activities more appealing, like jigsaw puzzles or searching with a UV torch. Teachers at a professional development session, on the other hand, can participate in teambuilding exercises that require solving tricky puzzles which require analytical thinking knowledge of many topic areas.

Breakout puzzles are best suited to practise factual knowledge and can be used in any subject that has key facts and definitions that students must memorise and apply to pass the course successfully. In the chapter on puzzle design, I have tried to cover a wide range of subjects in the examples, and at the end of each puzzle page, you can find a list of ideas for different subjects that might inspire you to find ways to incorporate it into your topic. Open-ended tasks like writing an analysis, creating a drawing or performing a dance routine are more challenging to incorporate as they do not all lead to the same outcome that can be turned into a code for a lock. An escape lesson can, however, serve as the starting point for analytical writing about the experience and the theme of the room can serve as inspiration for creative work. You can also incorporate shorter, open-ended tasks by stepping in as the game master who decides if a job has been performed well enough to earn the team access to the next challenge or passcode.

One of the main features in escape games is the time pressure that adds excitement and tension, and they are therefore best played as a one-off lesson. They are popular at the end of a term to keep the motivation going to the last minute, or to mark a special event in the calendar. If you want to include material for a more extended unit of work, I recommend a "quest" instead of an escape room. A quest is an overarching story that links each task in a series of lessons and connects them with recurring characters and themes. For example, I have created a murder mystery, where every page in the textbook ends with a challenge that gives students a clue to eliminate one of the suspects until they know who the murderer is and what their motive was. The website www.classcraft.com also offers ways of turning lessons into a kind of computer role-playing game and incorporating your lesson assignments into a quest map (some features are part of a paid-for subscription).

Escape games can be played with large numbers of students at the same time, but the number of students and the time and space available will, of course, have an influence on the types of activities you can include, and how to organise your session. If you have a larger class with little space, it might be best to opt for a digital escape room. A smaller group can be allowed more freedom to move around and choose the activities they prefer as it will be easier for the teacher to keep an eye on potential problems and to make sure everyone is engaged. In the chapter on example escape rooms, I describe a library induction escape room which was run for about 140 students in 5 sessions. This was only possible because we had a large space, the school library, available and each team had to complete the tasks in a different order so they would not get in each other's way.

With careful planning and playtesting, you will be able to make a game that all students in your group can enjoy, no matter how many there are and which ability level they have.

How do I plan the activity?

When planning your first escape room, you need to be aware that it will take longer to prepare than an ordinary lesson as you need to come up with a story, create the activities and then playtest the game. I would recommend starting at the weekend or in the holidays as it will be hard to plan in an afternoon. Before that puts you off, keep in mind that it will be a very special lesson that the students will not forget quickly and the activity can be re-used every year, including your puzzle items, if you store them carefully. Once you have created a fun escape room with a good story and enjoyable activities, it is relatively easy to adapt to different year groups and topics. I personally only run one or two escape room lessons with each class per year, so that the novelty does not wear off. Creating an escape room can also be extremely fun – I prefer creating puzzles over solving them as a brain challenge, and you can give your creativity full rein.

I will give a quick overview of the order of steps of planning a lesson here, but for each of the points, you can find more detailed advice in the following chapters.

Here are the steps:

1. Decide on the general topic and a storyline that complements it.
2. Taking into consideration the size and age of your group and the available space and devices, decide if you are going to create a physical, digital or mixed escape room and if a linear or non-linear setup is best suited.
3. Make a list of key concepts that the students need to learn or revise and bring them in a logical order. Try to mix more manageable revision tasks and more difficult new tasks that require some research to keep a balance between motivation and challenge.
4. Decide on the type of puzzles, using the suggestions in the puzzles chapter or your own ideas. Ideally include a mix of paper, digital and physical puzzles. Ensure you have a balance between puzzles that are based on short fact items, like dates and vocabulary, and puzzles that are more text-heavy or include other media like videos and sound files.
5. Start creating the puzzles using the templates and websites that can be found in the puzzle chapter.
6. While you are working on puzzles, make sure to write down the codeword or number that each activity will generate, especially if they need to be combined at the end to open the

final lock. If you are planning to share with other teachers, make sure you write down the answers to the puzzles as well.

7. Playtest with a small group of students if you can or with a colleague or friend. At the very least you should play through the whole activity yourself from start to finish and make sure all locks work and no puzzle pieces have been lost.

Here is an example table for planning an escape room for a languages lesson. The finished game had eight tasks for a 60-minute lesson for 13-year-old beginners. It is based on the topic of school, so the activities are based on different school subjects.

"room"	**topic**	**puzzle**	**resources**	**type**	**answers**	**code**
Biology	pets	code string	printout "code string", piece of string	match up	Hund=dog Katze=cat Maus=mouse ...	136
Sports	telling time	swimming race	digital	multiple-choice	Leo: 15min Tom: 45 min ...	17
Maths	numbers	jigsaw	printout "numbers", scissors	jigsaw puzzle, maths	3-1=eins 17+2=neunzehn...	80
English	family	cryptogram	printout "cryptogram", printout "answer key"	cryptogram	I have two brothers called...	29
END			**padlock on cupboard, prize**			**final code: 262**

How do I come up with a story?

What sounds more appealing: "We have to finish these five tasks by the end of the lesson to get through the chapter before the exam" or "We need to find five clues to uncover who murdered Sir John. We only have 60 minutes before the carriage arrives to take away the dinner guests"?

The story and the immersion are the main elements that set an escape room lesson apart from any old, boring lesson with some puzzles thrown in. Every part of your activity should tie in with your story – classroom decorations, worksheets layout and the types of puzzles you choose, so you need to work on the story before you go into too much detail in planning anything else.

When you decide on a story, the main question should be "If this was a film, would the students want to see it?" You have full choice of genre, and your story does not need to be realistic, it could even be set in the world of a famous book or film. If you enjoy storytelling, you can create an elaborate world with exciting characters and plot twists that are revealed bit by bit with every puzzle. If, however, creative writing is not your strong point, you need only about as much detail as you would find on the blurb of a book, just enough to create an intriguing atmosphere and link the puzzles together.

Looking at the topics you want to teach, a story might suggest itself: chemistry tasks offer themselves to CSI style investigations and history is by its very nature full of thrilling stories and shady characters. I have, for example, created an escape room for a French lesson based on the historical character of Le Comte de St Germaine, who was rumoured to be immortal. By researching his story, I found locations, documents and people associated with him that I could build into my story. Be careful though, some topics that make a good story might be deemed inappropriate by parents, students or colleagues. For example, "escape the concentration camp" or "escape the titanic" might be seen unsuitable as a game, especially if you are using the names or pictures of real-life victims. Other topics can also be sensitive issues for some children like "escape the asylum" or "prison break", even though these are common themes in real escape rooms.

If there is not an obvious link between your content and a story, you can find inspiration from commercial escape rooms. In 2018, Errol Elumir, a puzzle designer and host of the Escape Room Divas podcast, surveyed 562 adult escape room enthusiasts[2], the following themes ranked where in the top 10:

1. Tomb/Ancient Civilizations
2. Space
3. Historical
4. Supernatural
5. Science
6. Spy
7. Heist/Thieves
8. Dream
9. Crime/Police
10. Carnival

The study makes an interesting read if you want to find out why people enjoy escape rooms and what elements contribute to a fun experience.

---

[2] Elumir, Errol (2018) *2018 Escape Room Enthusiast Survey* <https://thecodex.ca/2018-escape-room-enthusiast-survey/>

Wikipedia[3] also has a list of common themes and stories that might give you ideas:

- Airplane
- Bomb Defusing
- Carnival
- Detective/Police/Crime
- Dream
- Heist / Thieves
- Historical
- Horror
- Library
- Medical / Asylum
- Military
- Magic
- Music
- Office
- Pirate
- Prison
- Science
- Serial Killer
- Sherlock
- Space
- Spy
- Supernatural

---

[3] Wikipedia: Escape Room, < https://en.wikipedia.org/wiki/Escape_room>

- Tomb / ancient civilization
- Vampire
- Western
- Zombie

If you are really stuck and do not have the time or inclination to write your own mystery, the website https://lockpaperscissors.co/mysterious-escape-room-themes/ offers "25 creative escape room themes you can use right now" in the form of a little story that could be an intriguing starting point to an escape room.

Whatever theme you go for, remember that it needs to include an exact time limit to explain why all the tasks have to be completed this lesson: "The spy has booked a flight in an hour, catch him before he escapes!" or "The volcano is about to erupt, find the map to the exit before the room gets covered in lava!".

What is the difference between linear and non-linear setup?

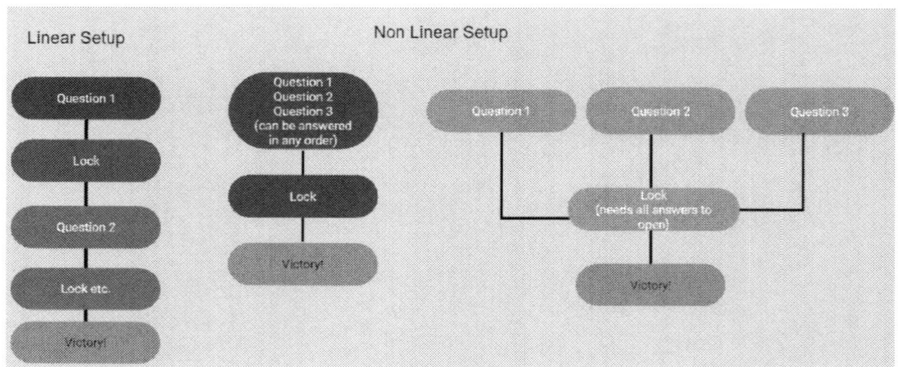

Image: Julia Morris

The choice between a linear or a non-linear setup is one of the first decisions you have to make before you go into planning your locks and puzzles. It determines if puzzles need to be solved in a particular order or if the students can choose which challenge to tackle first.

Linear setup

In a linear setup, the puzzles must be solved in a set order and solving a puzzle gives the students access to the next one. In a digital game, they move on by finding a link to the next page. In a physical game, they can receive a code for a padlock, get a hint where to find the next puzzle or be allowed access to a tool, like a pair of scissors or a torch, which they will need to complete the next task.

The linear setup is useful if the tasks have to follow a specific sequence to make sense, for example, if they are in chronological order like the plot of a book or the order of events on a historic day. A linear setup is also helpful if you want students to revise some basics before going on to more difficult tasks. Linear setups are easier to conduct as you know what steps the students have to take next and if the class runs out of time, you can help students skip steps to reach the goal quicker, or you can determine a winner by deciding who got the furthest.

On the downside, linear setups do not work well with larger groups as it usually is impractical for all of them to be working on the same question. In that case, you would need to split them into smaller teams, which in a physical escape room means buying multiple breakout boxes and locks, and it can make it expensive. Even when working in smaller groups, a linear setup means that the tasks cannot be shared out between the team members. That can be an advantage if you want to make sure teams work together on all tasks but can get annoying for students if one team member takes over and leaves the others with nothing to do. If one of the tasks is too difficult, students can get stuck, and if they are demotivated early on in the game, less confident students might be inclined to give up. It is therefore especially important in this setup that help is available to allow smooth progression from one task to the next.

Non-linear setup

In a non-linear setup, the questions can be answered in any order the final lock can only be opened when all the answers are found. The students have all the documents, puzzle pieces or web links right from the start and they can choose which to work on first. Digital escape rooms can be non-linear as well, by starting on a webpage with an overview that includes links to all tasks from which players can choose.

As you can see in the graph above, there are two different ways of organising a non-linear setup. The model in the middle shows students working in small teams: they decide together which question to answer first and use teamwork to solve them. Each puzzle gives them part of a passcode, and all the numbers together can be used to open the final lock.

The model on the right shows a whole class game in which different teams solve different puzzles simultaneously, and they only come together at the end to add up all their code for the final lock.

Non-linear games usually require more teamwork and communication as the students have to agree on the order of tasks, and they need to know when to share their results with the rest of the group. This is ideal if whole class team building is one of your aims but might require more teacher assistance in groups that are not used to this kind of working.

One advantage of playing a non-linear game is that you need fewer locks, even in bigger groups. You could get away with just one, which makes it cheaper and easier to set up. Keep in mind, however, that it also means that students have to do a lot more work before they get the satisfaction of successfully opening a lock.

For some students, this setup is more motivating as they can choose to work on the activities that they find the easiest or most fun. At the same time, it also means that they can avoid trickier tasks that would be useful for them to progress in their understanding of the topic.

If you are working with several locks in a non-linear setup, part of the challenge for the students could be to recognize which task fits which lock. The students start with a lot of different materials, like pictures, puzzles and other items, and have to work out themselves how to combine them and which of them are relevant and which are not. In a digital room, for example, the "lock" question could be simply "what is the date" without stating exactly where to find it or to which date it refers. In a physical room, it works best if you are using different types of locks, e.g. one needing letters, one numbers and one a key.

Multi-linear setup

A multi-linear setup is a mix of a linear and non-linear set-up. For example, the students can choose in which order to answer questions 1, 2, 3 and 4. Each will give them a digit for a 4-digit combination lock. Once they open the lock, they must solve question 5 to open a pair of scissors which they can use to cut a jigsaw puzzle for question 6 etc.

What is the difference between digital, physical and mixed escape rooms?

The choice between a digital, physical, mixed or even role-playing escape room, depends on the size of your group, the available time for preparation, the cost of equipment and the numbers of devices available.

Physical escape rooms

Physical escape rooms are most like commercial escape rooms in that there are real locks and items to handle, and students move freely around the room. They usually involve a number of different padlocks that need different types of codes. Often other things are in play too, for example, mirrors, UV torches, posters, statues and other props. The classroom can be decorated to resemble the fictional location and students walk around to manipulate objects and search locations. Each puzzle contributes to the overall aim (to escape the tomb, catch the murderer, etc.) and drives the narration forward.

This version is the most fun, as students enjoy the freedom to move and to play with objects. It is a lesson unlike any standard lesson, and students can explore the space and work on the puzzle that interests them most and speaks to their strengths. Turning a lock and hearing it click open is so much more satisfying that just ticking off a task in an exercise book and a puzzle piece that fits precisely into place can bring a lot of joy.

Unfortunately, an activity like this can also be quite tricky and expensive to organise and execute. The teacher or school might need to spend a considerable amount of money on hardware, especially if you need several sets. Ready-made sets of locks, boxes and puzzles available from www.breakoutedu.com , but they cost about $150 (including access to their online library of activities). To save money, many teachers create "imaginary" physical locks by turning a shoebox into a treasure chest or print an image of a lock that "opens" if the correct code is written onto it.

A physical escape room can be more challenging to control if you are working with a livelier group. It is also easier for some students to take over while others switch off if they are not allocated tasks in smaller teams. When working with larger groups, you either need several sets of each puzzle or enough different jobs to keep everyone occupied. In the latter case, students will have different experiences depending on what tasks they choose to work on, and not all of them will cover all the learning objectives.

A physical escape room requires a lot of preparation: even if the activities are mainly paper based, you will have to do printing, cutting and sticking to make it enjoyable. You will have to think about how to create an immersive environment in your room with displays and props (see "how can I make it more immersive?") and tables and chairs might have to be rearranged to make space. For these reasons, some teachers prefer the calmer, more orderly lessons that a digital escape room can facilitate.

Digital escape rooms

Digital escape rooms are typically based on an interactive presentation. The students click through the website or presentation, solving different puzzles to get to the next screen. The locks can consist of a click on certain parts of the screen with hidden links or by putting the answers in an online form, which will only provide the link to the next challenge if the input is correct.

The advantages of virtual escape rooms are that they can be created entirely for free and that they can be accessed by as many students as needed at the same time. Once the escape room is designed, you will need no other preparation, and it can be used last minute and easily shared with colleagues. A lot of different media like pictures, audio and video can be incorporated easily. There are no limits to your creativity, and you can create any kind of environment – it is much easier to find images of the "mysterious lab of the mad professor" than to turn your classroom into a convincing stage setting. You also do not have to worry about the physical constraints of your classroom as the students do not have to move around and will not need any extra space and there is no danger of a melee breaking out.

The disadvantage of digital escape rooms is that they are less immersive and depend on the availability of devices like computers or tablets for all students or teams. If students are using their own devices or if they are working from home, it might not be fair to give out a prize for the fastest players as a slow device or unreliable internet connection could be a considerable disadvantage. There is also a danger that each student will do the activity individually so that the team working element is lost. I would therefore make sure that a team of three works on a maximum of two devices, one for the escape room activity and one for research so they still need to collaborate and communicate.

Another problem is that some students spend too much time on screens already and many parents feel school should be a place where they do something else. Moreover, some teachers might think that it is difficult to keep up with the high level of digital game design that students are used to on their PlayStation at home and that they will not take the educational game serious. In my experience, however, students are generally impressed with the effort that has been spent on creating the activity and compare their escape room lesson favourably to their other, traditional classes, and do not expect it to be like the games they play in their free time.

Mixed escape rooms might be the answer to take advantage of the positives of digital activities while avoiding some of the problems.

Mixed escape rooms

In a mixed escape room, some or all of the story and the locks are digital, but some tasks are completed on paper or there are objects that need to be manipulated.

Personally, I prefer this mix: The main game is computer-based but students also have to handle some real-life objects, for example, a text wheel, a printed cryptogram or a stack of mysterious photos, to solve the challenges and open the digital locks. It is also fun to include some physical searching, e.g. a clue that gets them to look under their table to find a code number stuck there. I always try to lock up a special (edible) prize in my cupboard and the last challenge will tell them where to find the key to the cupboard, so the lesson often ends with a mad rush and a triumphant winning team. I always have to make sure there are some second prizes for the other teams to avoid disappointment!

In my experience, this type of escape room is the right balance between affordability and fun. I have played two very similar versions of an escape room with the same class of 17-year-olds, once as a mixed escape room and then again as a digital-only activity during remote learning. I felt that I had made some improvements in the digital version and the pictures and stories were more engaging. Surprisingly, the students said they still enjoyed the older, mixed version more because of the physical puzzles and the stronger social element. I had to realise that with so many educational games out there, an online game in itself is not that special to the students, it is the teamwork and the immersion in the story that makes it memorable.

If you are going for a mix between a website and paper resources, there are different options for organising them. If you give out all printed challenges at the beginning, it can be part of the task to work out which the resources are needed at what time. This is a good exercise in organisation and resource management, especially if there are a few "red herrings" in the form of mysterious items that are not actually going to be used. This way, some members of the team can start on one puzzle while others are working on a different activity which is easier done alone. If you prefer the tasks to be done in a specific order, make sure that the printout is missing an essential part for solving it that is only accessible online after completing other tasks first. Alternatively, you can put each puzzle in a numbered envelope which students can open when prompted to do so in the game. As a cheap alternative to envelopes, just use some plastic pockets with two sheets of paper and the puzzle hidden between them. If you want to make sure students stick to the order of the tasks, you can either lock up your resources and students have to find the code, or you walk around the class, giving out resources when they are needed.

The balance between the physical and digital parts are, of course, very flexible. Your activity could mainly involve tasks around the classroom, and the digital element is restricted to giving clues or checking answers. On the other extreme, your activity could take place entirely in a virtual world, with a few printed tasks. Once you have created your escape room, you can adapt the room depending on the classes or the demands on your time by printing some of the tasks or using the digital version instead. The chapter on puzzles provides a digital and a printed version for nearly all tasks. To avoid having to change your webpage each time, just add instructions like "Open envelope/file 1 to solve the puzzle" and hand out a stack of envelopes for a physical game or tell students the location of the files for the digital one.

Role-playing escape rooms

Role-playing escape rooms consist only of a story – all the action happens in the players' minds. To play these escape rooms, you will need a game master who has the script, similar to a "choose your own adventure" story, and all players take the roles of characters in the story. The game starts with a description of the room and the players can "search it" by asking "What do I find if I look under the bed" or "I would like to inspect the poster more closely". The game master then describes what they find, shows a picture or gives out a printout of the puzzle they have to solve. The game master can also give hints if the players get stuck and will tell them the consequence for each action.

A good example are the stories written by Dani Siller and Bill Sunderland for Escape this Podcast, https://www.consumethismedia.com/escape-this-podcast, and their scripts can be downloaded for free on their website. These escape rooms are great as they do not need any physical space and no computer skills. Still, to create your own, the teacher needs considerable creative writing skills and will need to anticipate all actions that the students might want to take or will have to improvise on the spot. I have not come across an educational version of a role-playing escape room, but I have used the Escape this podcast stories in my foreign language lesson by translating them into German. If you teach advanced English as a foreign language, they would be a great activity to do with your class.

A role-playing game can also be a great starting point for a creative and collaborative writing task if students are given time to write their own story. I have run an escape room club after school in which students played a few of the stories and then came up with their own scenario, items and puzzles so they could play the room with their friends. The students learned some valuable skills in the process, as they had to use creativity, communication and organisational skills. As you will see when you start planning your educational escape room, creating a puzzle requires just as much logic skills and can be just as fun as solving it!

What types of boxes and locks can I use?

It goes without saying that an escape room needs locks. You are probably not actually allowed to lock up a group of children in your classroom, so instead, breakout games in school are nearly always "break-in" games with students trying to get into one or several locked boxes to win the game. There are three different types of locks you can use, physical, digital and imaginary, and you can mix and match them as needed. As described in the chapter on mixed escape rooms, your puzzles could all be physical or paper-based, but the answer is put into a digital form to be checked, or your escape room can be mainly a computer game, but in the ends students find the code to a real-life lock, hiding a treasure.

Physical boxes and locks

When playing a physical escape room, you will want your students to solve more than one puzzle, so you either use lots of boxes, lots of locks on one box, or several puzzles that need to be combined to open a single lock.

If you are opting for one box with several locks, you could opt for a multi-lock hasp or lockout hasp which allows six or more padlocks to shut one box (see picture).

Image: Julia Morris

When playing with several locks, it is essential that it is obvious which puzzle opens which lock. Either your number the locks and the puzzles or, even better, include a mix of locks that require different input. You might be surprised how many types of padlocks there are- besides the standard locks with a key or a short number code, there are also padlocks with a dial, a letter passcode, a directional passcode or even a colour code. You can

Feeling a lock finally click open after solving a fiendish puzzle can be immensely satisfying but can be expensive to achieve for a whole class of 30 children, so we will look at a few solutions to this problem.

First, you should check with your school management if they would be happy to pay for a few sets of boxes and locks that can then be used by any teacher in the school – maybe offer to teach your colleagues about escape rooms in return!

If that strategy is not successful, take advantage of your environment. Most classrooms have cupboards and drawers that can be locked. It is, however, more challenging to organise all these different hiding places if you are playing in smaller teams because each team would need the chance to find each of the keys separately. A good place to play is a school library, as books are a great place to hide things because you can give out titles, page numbers and library classifications as clues and there usually is plenty of space to move around in.

If you want to play in teams and want each group to find the same code, it pays to think outside the box (literally!). For example, lock up the handles of a pair of scissors, a shoebox with a chain around it or put a padlock through some hole in an exercise book or ring binder. You could also ask colleagues or students to lend you lockable boxes like a money box, a jewellery box or even a piggy bank. If you are still struggling to create enough locked boxes, you could just use just one box and set of locks and let teams take turns in trying their code and then close the box again.

If you want to keep your spending at zero, you might have to go with imaginary or digital locks.

Imaginary locks

Imaginary locks are ones that could be opened at any time, but everyone pretends that a key is needed, e.g. a sealed envelope with a picture of a padlock on it. This is the simplest and cheapest way of creating locks, but it requires all participants to stick to the rules and not open anything too early. The codes are entered by writing them on the lock or saying them out loud and will require the teacher to check every code and give the go-ahead to open the lock. The teacher itself could act as the "lock": students need to bring their completed work or solved puzzle to them to receive the next challenge or hint.

The advantages of this way of playing, apart from the cost consideration and more straightforward setup, is that the teacher can keep a close eye on everyone's progress and give support when needed. It also means that tasks can be more open-ended and do not need to result in a precise passcode. For example, a picture of a nset could open the "lock" by presenting it to the teacher, so each team can have a different outcome and still progress in the game.

The main disadvantage, in my opinion, is that this is very similar to any standard lesson! It will be harder for students to be immersed in the game and for many students getting a thumbs up from the teacher is not quite as memorable and exciting as the satisfying clink of a lock opening. It also makes it tougher for you as the teacher as you will be busy checking work and making sure no one rushes ahead, and you will not have much time to support teams that are stuck or to observe their teamworking skills.

Some teachers, like Luke Rosa[4], have tried to find another solution by creating crossword-style escape game resources, where each puzzle leads to a codeword that needs to be entered in the boxes provided. When all answers are filled in, the highlighted boxes provide the final password. For example:

Solve task 3 to find out on what day of the week the murder took place:

Solve task 7 to find out the location:

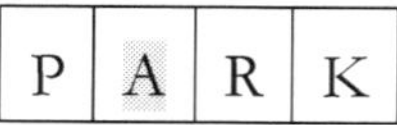

Solve task 8 to find out the time:

4 Rosa, Luke *Students of History Lesson Resources* <https://www.studentsofhistory.com/>

Take the highlighted boxes to find out who the murderer is and tell the police (your teacher) to claim a prize:

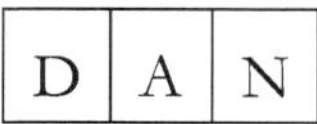

This way students get immediate feedback that their answer is right (if it fits in the boxes) and they can do the tasks in any order to reach their goal, although it does allow for some guessing.

Digital locks

Digital locks consist of a website or online form into which the correct answers are entered to get the next hint or to get to the next puzzle webpage. They have the advantage that they are completely free and do not need any space in the classroom. You can have as many different locks as you want and unlimited numbers of students using them at the same time. They check the answers automatically, and you can include links to further hints if students get stuck. They allow for a variety of responses, like words, sentences, numbers and multiple-choice. You can even create a kind of directional or colour lock by turning the code into letters (U=up; L=left or R=red B=blue, etc.). By using different pictures on your website or presentation, you can style the locks to fit your theme: the picture of a mouldy door in a haunted castle, a mysterious briefcase or a pirate chest.

The disadvantage is that they are less immersive and satisfying than real locks and can take the students out of the game, especially if the activity is set in an ancient tomb or something similarly low-tech. Depending on the facilities and rules in your school, it can also be difficult to get hold of enough internet-enabled devices for each group and to make sure that they use them sensibly. If students are using their personal devices, it can create unfairness because some are slower or run out of battery halfway through the game.

I prefer digital locks because they allow more variety and longer answers, however, my students often stumble over spelling mistakes and even an extra space or capital letter, which will prevent most digital locks from opening. Therefore, it is a good idea to include a hint telling them to check their spelling carefully. You will also have to include information on what kind of information needs to be entered (letters/numbers/words, how many digits, capital letters, punctuation) because it is not as obvious as with a real-life lock.

How do I create digital rooms and locks?

A good digital escape room consists of a website or presentation with pictures illustrating the story and a number of different challenges as well as several locks that need to be opened or checkpoints that must be passed.

In this chapter, I will present a few different options I have come across. The most useful is Lockee, so I will talk about that first. Then I will talk about the other options, starting from the easiest (and least exciting) to the more complex (and coolest). When reading about the various programmes, keep in mind that some of them are better as "rooms" to set the scene, while others are better as "locks" that require specific input. I will look at different Microsoft and Google products and at Genial.ly (a website for creating online presentations).

Feel free to mix and match them and even if you do not work at a "Google school" or a "Microsoft school", you can still make use of their tools, without having to create student accounts. All the Lockee, Genial.ly and Google tools are free and can be used in standard web browsers, while most of the Microsoft programmes work best when they are installed on your own and your students' devices, but can also be used in the web-based version of Office, but will require a Microsoft subscription.

Lockee

The website https://en.lockee.fr/ offers the option to create a variety of online locks that can hide a number of types of media that can be accessed via a link or embedded in a website like Genial.ly or Google sites and it even automatically generates a QR code for each lock that can be displayed or printed and then scanned to access the lock with a mobile device.

This is from the website itself: "It is possible to create the following locks:

- Digital: you must type the code on a numeric keypad;
- Directional: you must type the code on a directional keyboard (top, bottom, left, right);
- With colours: you have to type the code on a keyboard with colours;
- Musical: you must type the code on a piano keyboard (including a scale);
- With pattern: it is necessary to draw a path on a grid including nine points;
- With switches: Flip the correct switches.
- Geotagged: you have to move and use the location of the device;
- Username / Password: you must enter a username and password (text fields);
- Password: you must enter a password (text field).

Image: https://en.lockee.fr/faq/

The following contents can be displayed after opening a lock:

- a text: a text with formatting (bold, underlining, colours) that can contain links;
- an image: an image uploaded from your device directly hosted on the site;

- a sound file: a sound uploaded from your device directly hosted on the site;
- an external video: a video hosted on an external site (Youtube, Dailymotion, Vimeo);
- a webpage: a redirection to an external web page."[5]

All these different options make Lockee very versatile and easy to use. You will need to create a free account, but students will not have to sign up. By default, users are limited to creating and storing 30 locks, but you can ask for more by emailing the teacher who runs the site – details can be found in the FAQ section. As the locks are hosted on the website, you can easily incorporate them into a physical escape room by printing the QR codes. If you are running a digital escape room, a great feature is that you can create the locks without a background, so it is easy to superimpose them over background pictures to make the part of your story. Since you can hide text behind the locks, it can be used to give out passcodes for real-life locks or the password for a password-protected file. A web link can be used to give access to the next Google Site page or to the next Genial.ly presentation page. Here is an example Genial.ly presentation with three different locks. On the last page, you can also find a link to a S'cape tool that allows you to find the URL for an individual Genial.ly page.

Word documents

Most teachers and students will be familiar with Microsoft Word and how to create worksheets with them, so it is an easy starting point for designing an escape room, simply by adding password protection to your work. In Word, go to "File" – "Info" – "Protect document" and

[5] https://en.lockee.fr/faq/

choose a password. It cannot be recovered, so make sure to write it down somewhere.

Now you can create a chain of documents: Create a puzzle worksheet and give it to the students. The answer to the puzzle will be the password to the first protected document, which itself contains another puzzle that leads to a password for the next document and so on.

Word is an easy option for paper-based puzzles, but it does not make a very immersive room. To create a more exciting atmosphere, you either combine it with a presentation or website, or you could try to spin a story around it, for example, "You have managed to break into the super villain's house and are trying to find information about his evil deeds on his computer, but everything is password protected. Luckily, he left himself a password reminder on a note on his desk..."

Google documents

As far as I know, you cannot password protect Google documents, but you can give the students an incomplete link to a document. Instead of working out the password, they have to work out the numbers and letters missing from the link to be able to open the document. To do that, create the document, click "share" and change it "anyone with the link". Then copy the link and take a few letters out like in the example below.

https://docs.Google.com/presentation/d/ ___ ___ ___ ____xdxyy8PjWCDtWAmhrBnZ-oQ6w7Wv_W0ly3TPoyQ/edit?usp=sharing.

Like Word documents, Google documents are best combined with a presentation or website to make it more into an escape room and less a standard lesson.

Google slides

Google slides allow you to add images, animations and videos. Unfortunately, unlike PowerPoint presentations, they do not offer any settings to stop students from skipping a task and going straight to the next slide. Google slides escape rooms will therefore only work if you either have control over the presentation (i.e. you play it as a whole class activity) or if the group commits completely to the game and promises to solve all tasks. A way of avoiding skipping ahead is to embed individual slides into a Google site (see below). You could also break up the presentation into smaller chunks, and at the end of each, they have to "unlock" a Google form which gives them access to the next production (see below how to do that).

OneNote

A popular tool for escape rooms is OneNote as each section in your notebook can be password protected separately. This means that you do not end up with lots of different documents or presentations, but you can still stop students from accessing the next scene until they have found the code. OneNote is also an excellent tool because you can embed all kinds of media like worksheets, presentations, videos and Genial.ly presentations.

To add a password, just right click on a section and choose "password protect section". Using OneNote also has the advantage that you can check students' progress if you have set up the class, and each student has their own section. Students can solve puzzles within OneNote, and you, as the teacher, can go into their Notebook, check what they have done and give them live feedback even if they are working at home. In OneNote, they also have a place to keep their work for later reference, and even if they are working as a team, it is easy to make copies of the sections for each team member.

Google Forms

Google forms are a great tool to create locks and can be embedded in Google Sites or Genial.ly presentations and linked from Word documents or PowerPoints. Do not dismiss Google forms, just because your school is not officially a Google school – your students will not need a Google account to fill them in, although you will need one to create it. Google forms have one distinct advantage over Microsoft forms: they allow "response verification" which means you will only be able to progress if the correct word is filled in. Microsoft forms have a branching option that gives you different feedback, depending on your answers, but only in multiple-choice questions, so they are not as useful as "locks".

Here is my video on how to create a Google form lock: https://youtu.be/42JQQXIvH7A.

These are the steps:

- Enter "forms.new" into your web browser address bar. This will create a new form automatically.
- Enter your question, e.g. "What is the code" and choose "short answer" from the drop-down menu.
- Turn on "required" – this means students cannot progress without filling this part in.
- Click the three dots and choose "response validation."
- Next to the answer, there are now two new dropdown menus. Choose "regular expression" and "matches" and enter your code or solution in the field that says "pattern".
- Make sure to fill in the "custom error text". This will appear if a partial answer or the wrong answer is entered. Write in here how many numbers or letters are required, as well as any capital letters or punctuation. You could also add a hint on where/how to find the answer.

- Now add another section. In the picture above, it is the bottom symbol on the right-hand side. Students will only see what is in the next section after they have entered the correct answer(s) in the first section.

- If you are using a non-linear way of playing, you can enter all questions in the first section. This gives students the choice to answer the questions in whatever order they like. For a linear setup, enter one question per section, so they have to solve the challenges in this particular order.

- In the next section, enter the text that will take students to the next challenge, e.g. a link to a worksheet/website/presentation or a clue where they can find the next paper-based puzzle. If this is the last challenge, it could simply say "You won!" or "tell your teacher, the codeword .... to claim your prize".

Here is an extra trick: for the students, the second section will look something like this:

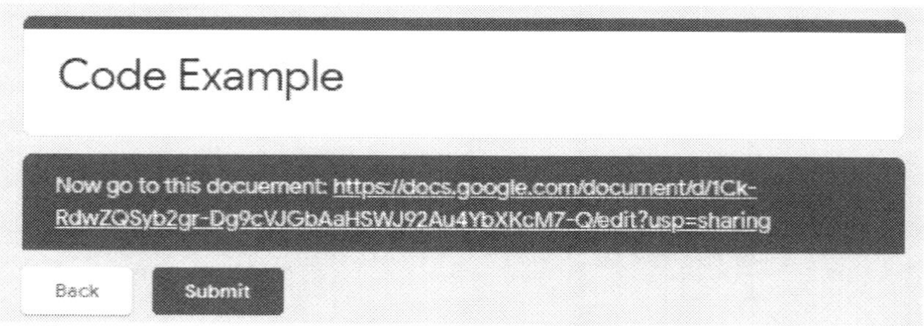

In my experience, students often make the mistake that they click "submit" instead of following the link – they get a "thank you" and cannot go back to the link unless they fill in the form again from the beginning.

To avoid this problem, add another section, but you do not need to write anything in it. In between this last section and the one above, there is a dropdown menu that says "after section 2 continue to next section" (or similar). Change it to say "after section 2 continue to section 2". This creates a loop which means students cannot submit the form which will hopefully help them realise that they must use the hint or link instead. The disadvantage is that you cannot use the form as a checkpoint to see how far students have come because they cannot submit it.

Google Sites

Google sites are a straightforward and free tool to create websites that can act as "rooms". You will need a Google account to make them, but not to use them. The advantage of a Google site is that each page in the site has its own web address that can be "discovered" by solving a puzzle.

Type "sites.new" into your web browser to get started. You can now include pictures, texts, forms, videos and embed learningapps and Genial.ly activities. After you have created several pages, go to the page list on the right and click the three dots next to the slide name and choose "hide from navigation". Now, the only way to get from one page to another is to find a direct link to it, either hidden in a picture or as a reward after opening a Google form lock.

PowerPoint

Using PowerPoint and Genial.ly allow you to present a story with interesting graphics and animations and to add many different types of content, like videos and links to other websites. PowerPoint will be more familiar to most teachers and is, therefore, an easy starting point. When you feel more confident in designing an escape room activity, it is worth looking into Genial.ly as it offers some additional options and more flexibility.

If you use the standard PowerPoint settings, you will have the same problems as with Google slides, namely that it is easy to go to the next slide or enter editing mode without solving the puzzles. Here is the trick to solve this problem: Create your presentation and in the "slide show" tab, click "set up slide show", then select "browse at kiosk". Next, go into the "transitions" tab, and make sure "on mouseclick" is checked. When you have finished designing the presentation, save it as a "PowerPoint Show (ppts)" and share the file with the students. Now it will automatically start in present mode, and you can only forward the slide if a certain area is clicked.

You can add a link to the next slide to any object on the page, by using right-click and "link". For example, letters on a keyboard or the numbers on a calculator can take you to the next slide, if you add them as individual objects. Number keypads that have letters on the buttons can also be used to enter words (template here). In the example below, the first number of the code is 4, so it has a link to slide 2, where the next code number has to be entered. All other numbers should be linked to a slide saying "wrong code" with a time delay (see in puzzle design chapter) to avoid guessing. More details on how to create invisible clickable areas can be found in the puzzle chapter under "Hidden objects."

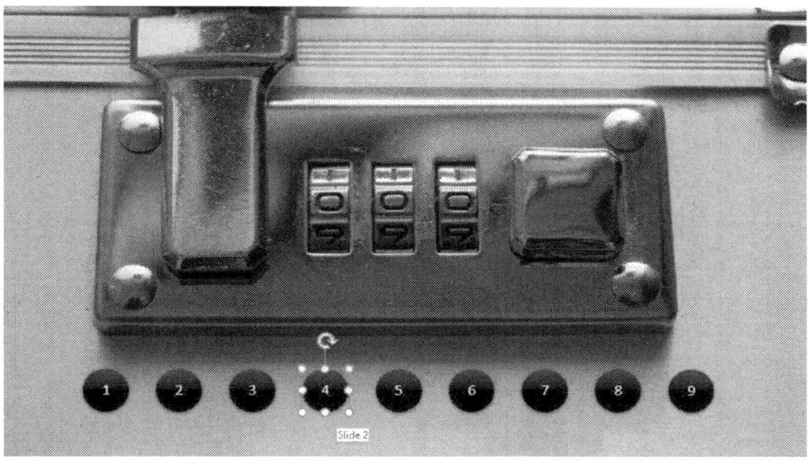

Image: Genial.ly

Genial.ly

Genial.ly is a relatively new website for creating presentations, but it has quickly established itself as a firm favourite with teachers making escape rooms. Using the Genial.ly website, you can create presentations that are designed to be viewed online, without a student log-in and without needing access to any software or apps. It offers a great range of stock images, as well as many templates, specially designed for escape room activities. Some require a paid account, but most are free, and you can create very slick looking escape rooms with the basic, free account. Here is one of the free templates: https://view.Genial.ly/5f6740fa51337070914e426e/game-breakout-mystery-breakout-template. Reuse it by clicking the blue button at the bottom.

Two important advantages over PowerPoint are the possibility of moving items across the slide while in presentation mode and being able to view the presentation in any web browser on any device.

In Genial.ly it is also easier to avoid skipping ahead, simply change the settings to a "microsites" so arrows to the next slide are disabled. Adding invisible links is much quicker than in other presentations, too: click "interactive elements" and "invisible area".

Genial.ly, unlike PowerPoint, also allows embedding objects with an embed code, including YouTube videos, learningapps and Google forms. Genial.ly activities themselves can also be embedded in Google sites and OneNote pages. It has some other nice features like "tool tips" – little pop-up windows which can be used to give extra hints or translations. You can make items draggable, which is great for searching the slide with "UV lights" or moving objects around to get a code.

The newest feature in Genial.ly is that it allows you to password-protect individual slides – perfect for escape room locks! Simply click the three dots next to the slide preview on the left to add a password.

Image: Genial.ly

It is a pity, though, that at the moment the page asking for the password cannot be modified much: you can only choose the question (e.g. "What is the password?"), the password and the background colour, but you can't add any pictures. That means you either need to use the S'cape tool (see below) or, if you want to add an image of a lock like in the briefcase example, each number of the lock will need a separate slide and you have to add extra slides for "error" messages for each. As creating each lock takes times, it is easier to give students several tasks where they have to collect numbers that need to be added up to open a single lock at the end. In this type of game setup, I like adding a Google form (in the picture above it can be found in the eye icon), so students can use it to check all their answers and pinpoint where they might have made a mistake, so they do not have to replay the whole game.

If you would like to watch a video introduction to Genial.ly escape rooms, I recommend the webinar by Carmen Quirós: https://youtu.be/zjx4oqFAsZM?t=112. For additional puzzle and design ideas, have a look at my video here: https://youtu.be/vJDjDVY2DFE

S'cape

S'cape, https://scape.enepe.fr/, is a website about educational escape rooms that offers a lot of great puzzle templates and ideas, including several codes that can be added to a Genial.ly presentation to give it more functionality. Unfortunately, at the moment the website is only available in French, but Marie Allirot, a fellow language teacher, and I have translated a lot of the instructions and collected them in a Genial.ly presentation that can be found here: https://view.Genial.ly/5f3ba271df60d90d8a0efda6/interactive-content-scape-tools-for-Genial.ly

One of their most useful tools allows you to insert text boxes as password check into your slide and when the correct answer or code is entered, a text, picture or link to the next slide appears. Use the instructions and templates in this presentation to add this tool to your Genial.ly presentation: https://view.Genial.ly/5f45700679b77d0d928170cb/interactive-content-quiz. More information and instructions about how to use the other tools on the site can be found in the chapter on Learningapps, Bookwidgets and S'cape.

What is good puzzle design?

Once you have decided on your story and what types of locks you are going to use, you need to tackle the most important task: Creating puzzles.

In a commercial escape room, the main consideration for the designer is to make it as fun and as immersive as possible within the constraints of the available budget and technology. They want their customers to feel the room was worth the money and to come back and play one of their other rooms. When designing an educational escape room, other factors come into play, like the number of students in the class, the teacher's available time to spend on preparing and the subject content. The fun factor is not necessarily the main focus, even if it is still important. Before you start planning your challenges, it is good to be aware of the ideas behind good puzzle design, even if we cannot always meet all demands in a classroom setting.

Scott Nicholson is a Professor of Game Design and Development at Wilfrid Laurier University in Brantford, Canada and is the international research authority on escape rooms, including their use in education. He has written many papers and articles on puzzle design; the two most interesting ones for our context are "Ask why"[6]

---

[6] Nicholson, Scott (2016) *Ask Why: Creating a Better Player Experience Through Environmental Storytelling and Consistency in Escape Room Design* <http://scottnicholson.com/pubs/askwhy.pdf>

and "Creating engaging escape rooms for the classroom"[7]. To summarize, he recommends looking at each puzzle in an escape room and ask why it has been included. If the answer is "because it is a fun puzzle that I wanted to try out" or "it is a topic the students need to learn about" then it is not good enough – it also has to make sense within the narrative of the room and has to develop the story. For example, using a calculator to solve a complicated equation in an ancient Egypt themed room does not make much sense, but solving an equation that a spy has used to encrypt a secret message will allow the players to stay within the story. Every object they use should be part of the story and explain the action for example "You have found this calculator in the bag left behind by the maths genius when he was kidnapped by the evil co-operation to stop him revealing their shady business dealings."

Nicholson is also a proponent of including moral dilemmas and choices into your escape game: "Because live-action games engage the player directly with the game, they provide an opportunity to engage the player in the story behind the game. These games can have elements where the players have to make a choice with implications, and by doing so, create moments where the player is involved in affecting the storytelling experience." If the aim of the

---

[7] Nicholson, Scott (2018) *Creating engaging escape rooms for the classroom*. Childhood Education 94(1). 44-49. <http://scottnicholson.com/pubs/escapegamesclassroom.pdf

game is to find a hoard of money stolen in a heist, students are asked to reflect carefully at the end what to do with the money. Will they return it to the bank, keep it for themselves or spend it on a good cause? Or they might find out that a politician has manipulated an election, but only to avoid a dictator coming into power, will they keep the secret or reveal all? There are no right or wrong answers to these questions and winning the escape room should not depend on the answer. Instead, they should be the starting point for an ethical or philosophical discussion in the de-briefing session that could be continued into the following lessons. The teacher can have different ends to the story prepared, depending on the choices the class or the team makes, each highlighting the consequences of their actions or the class could even write different endings themselves to reflect on it further.

When deciding on the order of your activities, it is good to be aware of the two different types of challenges: puzzles and tasks. Puzzles require brainpower, concentration and subject knowledge and often the most challenging part of the puzzle is to work out how to go about solving it. For those types of puzzles, it is important to make very clear to the students that this is part of the challenge, so they do not get frustrated by the lack of instructions. Include a title like "If only we knew what these numbers mean...", so students know it is up to them to figure it out. Tasks, as opposed to puzzles, are activities that are straightforward but take time or skill. Tasks can be stand-alone challenges, for example, a jigsaw puzzle, a maze or a search with a UV torch, or they can be combined with a puzzle. For example, students have to solve the puzzle of a text with some numbers underneath. It might take them a while to realise that the numbers indicate which word and which letter to take to form a password. Once they have solved the puzzle part by understanding the connection between the numbers and the text, it becomes a task, as they have to simply count words and letters and note them down.

A well-designed escape room activity needs to prevent winning by guessing. Hopefully, most students will buy into your story and enjoy the game, but you might still have some who just want to get through it as quickly as possible, either to claim a prize or because they "can't be bothered". The greatest danger here are multiple-choice questions, especially digital ones, because students will be much quicker at guessing randomly between 4 options than thinking about the problem. Add as many options as possible to multiple-choice puzzles and make sure codewords or phrases are not obvious after finding only half of the letters.

In digital games, it is advisable to add a time penalty for wrong answers, one that is so boring that students rather do some research than sit through a minute of watching a ticking clock – even 15 seconds can feel like an eternity! If you are using Genial.ly or PowerPoint to create your escape room, the wrong answers should take students to a slide that give them some kind of feedback, maybe even a hint how to solve it and a time-delayed "try again" button that takes them back to the task. To do that, add an animation to your button, so it only appears after a certain time, between 5 and 15 seconds is probably enough. With some types of digital puzzles, you need to keep in mind that students might click the wrong place by mistake because the clickable areas are very small or very close together. In that case, add less time penalty to keep frustration to a minimum, but use a longer time penalty for a straightforward multiple-choice quiz with only three or four answers.

What puzzles can I use?

The key to your choice of puzzles and their order is variety. Try to mix:

- the type of puzzle - from jigsaw puzzle to code wheel
- the medium used - videos, text or digital task

- the level of difficulty of the content – revision or new concepts
- the difficulty of the puzzle itself – how obvious is it what to do and how long will it take

It is difficult to give guidance on how many puzzles to use as it depends on the group and the level of challenge of the tasks. I have found that around eight seems to be a good number for a one-hour lesson to make sure there is time for an introduction and for most teams to finish.

The difficulty level of the content and the puzzle type need to be balanced carefully: more complex subject content should be practised with more straightforward tasks, and more manageable revision tasks can be part of a puzzle that takes longer to figure out. This way, the overall challenge is not too great in any of the activities. If your room is based on a new topic, try to avoid too much reading as this will take the students out of the game. Instead, break the material into lots of smaller chunks. If the topic is too complex to do that it might not be a good idea to introduce it with an escape room – keep the excitement of the game for a revision session instead. Another way of avoiding too much reading is to mix tasks based on texts, words, videos and sound, if possible.

With more difficult content, think carefully how much of an activity the students need to do before they get some kind of feedback that they are on the right track. A crossword puzzle, for instance, gives instant feedback - either the word fits, or it does not. Digital puzzles also normally provide immediate feedback for a wrong click. However, if the students have to answer a long list of questions and then have to add all answers together to get the passcode, there is a danger that they will get frustrated if the code is not correct because they do not know which of their answers was wrong or if they have just added it up incorrectly. In the classroom, the teacher can provide guidance, but if it is a digital activity, I recommend adding a form with answer validation (see in "Locks") so students can check where they have gone wrong.

If you want students to acquire knowledge during your escape room, you will need to allow students to research, either online or in textbooks. You should, however, keep in mind that they will not want to spend a lot of time on in-depth study if there is a price for the fastest team. I always allow students to do online research, even if it is a revision topic because this way everyone can participate no matter what their previous knowledge level is, and they can check their own mistakes if they get stuck.

How can I make it more immersive?

One of the top reasons why escape room enthusiasts enjoy the experience is the immersion: they can forget their real surrounding, become part of the story and take on a new persona. Immersion and storytelling are also what sets your escape room lesson apart from a regular lesson with some puzzles. Of course, teachers cannot spend as much time and money on decorating their room as commercial escape rooms, but there are ways of making the students curious to find out more and drawing them into the story.

Immersion has several different elements to it. First, students need to be introduced to the story and the goal of the activities. If you are a good actor and narrator, then reading out the introduction might be enough to draw them in. A PowerPoint presentation could provide pictures in the background while you are speaking and help you to structure it. Alternatively, you could let the pupils discover the story themselves by hanging up posters, maps, fake newspaper articles and wanted posters and giving them time to explore their surroundings. To create more of a buzz, you might want to put up some of the posters a few lessons before the actual game lesson to get students guessing what might happen.

Personally, I like starting the game with a video introduction, and they are easier and quicker to create than you might think. Websites like www.powtoon.com and www.animoto.com offer easy to use templates, and you can just upload a few pictures, add some text, and the website will provide the animations and music to make it look professional. If you are working on an iPad or Mac, you could make a "trailer" with iMovie. A video catches everyone's attention and the pictures, the cuts and especially the music set the tone and create excitement.

The second and most crucial factor to immersion is in how far all puzzles and tasks are linked to the story and carry the narrative on instead of just being a task that needs to be ticked off, as we have seen in more detail in the chapter on good puzzle design.

A third element helping students to feel part of the story are authentic (or authentic looking) props. If you are planning your escape room far enough in advance, you might have time to rummage around some second-hand shops or ask friends and family to lend you items with connections to history or far off places. A simple wooden box or a fancy looking jewellery box can make the perfect treasure chest and an African mask or a microscope could be great decorations to pique the students' interest. If you cannot lay a hand on real items, just fake it! It is incredible (and slightly worrying) how easy it is to fake everything, from shopping receipts to text messages, from plane tickets to newspaper headlines. Here is a list of some websites you can use:

- fake concert tickets: http://www.faketicketgenerator.com/
- fake newspaper clippings and clapper boards: https://www.fodey.com/generators/newspaper/snippet.asp

- fake newspaper headlines: https://newspaper.jaguarpaw.co.uk/
- fake plane tickets: http://omatic.musicairport.com/
- fake ransom notes: http://www.ransomizer.com/
- fake shopping receipts: http://www.fakereceipt.us/sales_receipt.php
- fake signs: http://www.addletters.com/
- fake texts message: http://iphonefaketext.com/
- fake WhatsApp messages: http://www.fakewhats.com/

Fake emails or skype messages can also be easily generated by using your own account and a non-existent email address as the sender.

All these fake documents can be used as decoration around the room or as part of your introduction presentation or of a puzzle. I like mixing real and fake pictures, some relevant, some not, like in the example below. Part of the puzzle here is to work out which pictures will be needed and with which activity they need to use. If you are running a physical escape room, you can either print the pictures all on one page or hide them or hang them up around the room. For digital games, include a picture of a top-secret folder, a chest or a bookshelf that will take them to the collection of mysterious pictures when clicked.

Image: Julia Morris

Everybody knows that it is the music that makes horror films so scary, so make use of it to create the right atmosphere in your classroom. Type your theme (e.g. "spy music") into your favourite music player, like YouTube, Spotify or Amazon Music, and you will probably find a ready-made playlist. If you do not have a subscription to a music service, maybe one of your students is happy to play the music from their device, or you will have to be quick to turn down the sound when the adverts come on so that the students are not distracted.

Elliot Baily runs the https://lockpaperscissors.co/ escape room company, and he has several Spotify playlists to go with his escape game kits that you can find here: https://open.spotify.com/user/elliottjbailey. Equally, the YouTube Channel "Oldstuff4all" https://www.youtube.com/user/oldstuff4all/videos has a great choice of compilations like "music for doing magic" and "music for reading horror stories" and you can even find "30 minutes of ticking clock". My personal favourite on YouTube is the "60 min deluxe timer" https://www.youtube.com/watch?v=UiS9LMziSt8&t=2s with ticking sounds and announcements of the remaining time – it really has everyone at the edge of their seats and if you only need 40 minutes, can simply skip forward and start from a later point in the video.

How do I organise the lesson and timing?

The most important question when creating your first escape room is "How many puzzles do I need to plan for my lesson?" Unfortunately, it is very hard to say as it depends on the difficulty of the puzzles, the amount of content they need to research and the motivation of the students – the bigger the prize, the quicker the students! You also need to ask yourself if you want the game to continue all lesson or do you want even the slowest team to be able to solve everything in time, so they do not feel frustrated by having to leave the story unfinished. In the latter case, make sure to prepare extension tasks for the students who finish first. As a rough guide, I normally use about seven to nine puzzles for a 60 min lesson to give most teams time to reach the end. If you want to be on the safe side, plan a lot of puzzles and when the end of the lesson nears, and no team has won yet, give out more hints or allow them to skip a few puzzles.

Here is a sample structure of a breakout lesson:

1. Students arrive and are put into teams.
2. Introduce the setting by telling them the story or showing a video, pictures or props.
3. The timer is started, and all teams start at the same time.
4. Students work in teams. The teacher is available to answer questions but should stay in the background as much as possible.
5. One team wins and gets some recognition or prize if it is played as a competition.
6. Students who have finished the task, complete extension work while other teams are finishing.
7. Optional de-brief.

Teamwork is an essential part of an escape game, and it is worth spending some time thinking about how to facilitate it. In my experience, teams of three work best, as they can all see the screen or the resources at the same time and they do not have to wait long to get something to do if they are taking turns. As every teacher knows, there are many ways of grouping students into teams: in friendship groups, mixed ability, by working style or completely random. For escape rooms, especially competitive ones, mixed ability teams are a good choice: this way it is less likely that one team will be much fast than the others or that a whole team completely switches off or gets distracted by chatting. I have been surprised in the past that some students who struggle with the subject in normal lessons get drawn in by the puzzles and work much better than normal. In an ideal case, they are paired with someone who excels at the subject content to help them solve the challenges. It might be worth conducting a little survey beforehand to ask students who if they are keen puzzlers or who like to play puzzle-apps on their phone to make sure they are spread equally between the teams.

Once you have put students into teams, set a timer and start the activity. It is difficult for most teachers but try to hold yourself back and not give too much help – the students need to have time to discuss and try different solutions. We will look more into giving hints in the next chapter.

When it comes to celebrating success, there are not just differences between teachers but also between countries. In the UK, competition is generally seen as a valid way of motivating and a good preparation for "real life", while in Germany, students are encouraged to work collaboratively, and the success of one should not make another student feel like a failure. Depending on your attitude to competition, you can reward individual students, teams or the whole class by giving prizes or praising them. In many commercial rooms, teams can have their picture taken holding "We got out!" signs and if your school policy allows, you could do the same and display the photo in school or on social media.

Some educators feel that the de-briefing session after the game is an essential part of the activity. It allows the students to reflect on difficulties and highlights of the tasks and of working in a team. They can discuss any ethical choices they had to make as part of the story and can give the teacher feedback on which parts were the most enjoyable or most educational and what could be changed to avoid future problems.

How do I give hints?

Our first instinct as teachers when we see a student struggling or making a mistake is to step in, give explanations and solutions. It can, therefore, be very hard for the teacher just to watch as students are trying different methods to overcome a challenge in the escape game. Depending on what your normal lessons look like, it might also feel unnatural just to sit and watch and not be as actively involved in the work going on, but considering that you have spent all this work on preparing this unique lesson, just relax, you have earned it! It is also a vital part of the process for students to encounter obstacles and solve them by using their logic, subject knowledge and communication skills. Having a clear hint system with a limited number of hints available can help the students to build up resilience and independence, and it can also help the teacher to stop themselves from interfering.

If you are using a hint system, it needs to be established and explained with the introduction of the story and all need to agree to stick to it. It is often tricky to anticipate what kind of questions the students will have, so the easiest way is to give out cards with "hint" printed on them or other tokens that can be swapped for help from the teacher. For example, in a pirate-themed room, each team is given three gold coins that can be used to pay the "pirate grandpa" (played by the teacher) to give them some advice.

Another method is to give an unlimited amount of hints, but teams get a time penalty of one minute with every hint they use if the game is played as a competition. If there is no competitive element, students could "buy" the hints in another way, for example by reciting a poem or the 6x table.

To help students stay in the flow of the story, it is best if the hints can be built into the theme, like the pirate example above. The way the hint is given could also reflect the theme: in a historical setting, questions and answers need to be written out and delivered as letters, in a modern spy hunt, hints are sent by text message or written as emails. Imagine how much fun it would be if you could organise someone else to give the hints by sliding notes under the door or over walky-talky!

Some teachers might worry that a hint system would not work in a mixed-ability class, and in those circumstances, you might need to be a bit more lenient with your system. To make it feel fair to everyone, you should insist on all team "paying" the same amount for a hint, but how detailed your clue is, is entirely up to you. The other groups will probably not even notice if you give more concrete instructions to students who are struggling.

Can I see an example?

In the last chapter of this book, I will go through two full-length examples in detail, but if you would like to play through a short example yourself, use the links below and see if you can find Bigfoot within 15 minutes! This activity is a quick escape room that I have created for training purposes, and I have chosen topics that I hoped most of my colleagues did not know much about so they had to do some online research to put themselves in the students' place.

There are three ways of playing this activity. To save writing out the individual addresses, use the link collection:

http://bit.ly/morrisescape

1. As a digital activity, using a Genial.ly presentation
2. As a digital activity, using Google sites, Google forms, PowerPoint and Excel
3. As a mixed media activity: use the Google link but print the worksheet and the second slide of the PowerPoint and cut it out to create the wheel decoder.

PART 2: PUZZLES

The following part of this book is a collection of puzzle ideas that can be used in your escape room. Nearly all of them are suitable for a physical or in a digital escape room, and whenever possible, I have included a link to a template or website that helps you to create the activity. I have only included activities that can be linked with subject content in some way and have provided examples from different subjects that might inspire you to find a way of using the puzzle with the topic you are planning to teach. Each chapter will show you what the puzzle looks like, how to create it and how to solve it.

How do I use the templates?

All templates have downloadable templates or links to webpages that allow you to create the task online. All the digital content can be access through the short link and QR code at the end of the book.

For most tasks, I have included a Genial.ly template, as well as a PowerPoint or Word template uploaded on my Google drive. This way, they can easily be converted into a Google file. Please note that the preview in Google often does not show accurately what the presentation will look like if opened in PowerPoint or Google slides.

To open the templates, click the link while holding down CTRL or copy and paste the link in a web browser. If you would like to use it in Microsoft Office, click the download button. To use the files in Google, do not download them, but click "Open with Google slides/sheets/docs" and it can then be edited and saved in Google drive, either as a ppt (PowerPoint) or converted into a Google file.

Genial.ly works slightly different from PowerPoint or Google Slides, so the activity templates are not necessarily identical, but the Genial.ly activities often look better. Unfortunately, the links sometimes trigger a safety warning on Windows, so you might have to copy and paste them into the address bar instead of just clicking the link. Open the Genial.ly page and try out the activity. Click "Reuse this Genial.ly" at the bottom. You will then be prompted to sign in to your (free) account. You can now edit this template and use it as a stand-alone activity or add it in another website by clicking "All set" in the top right corner. It will then give you the option to share with a link or with an embed code (in the "insert" tab). If you want the activity to be part of a digital Genial.ly escape room, go into your presentation, click "add page" and chose "My creations" on the left. Next, find the presentation with my template and choose which slides you want to import. Genial.ly works well on any internet-enabled device without needing to download an app, so you could even incorporate it in a mainly physical escape room by including a QR code to the activity.

How do I make the code fit my lock?

As we have seen in a previous chapter, there are many different locks, digital and physical, and some require numbers, some letters and some even directions to open. When looking at the library of puzzles below, you might want to try a text-based puzzle, but you need it to open a 4-digit padlock – what do you do? Here are a few tricks on how to "convert" puzzle answers into codes.

The answer is a word, but I need a number or vice versa

Option 1 Count the letters: The most straightforward way to turn a word into a number is to simply count the letters in the word. This will typically give you only a single-digit number, so students might have to solve several puzzles to get to a longer code number.

Option 2 First letters: Similarly, if you have numbers and need letters, use the first letters of each number.

Option 3 Code key: Give students a key to turn the word into a number, e.g. A=1, B=2, etc., so the word CAT would give you the number 3 1 20.

Option 3 Tables: Create a table with possible answers, either as words or as pictures. The students need to find the answer to the puzzle in the grid to get the right number(s).

Example1: pictures to numbers

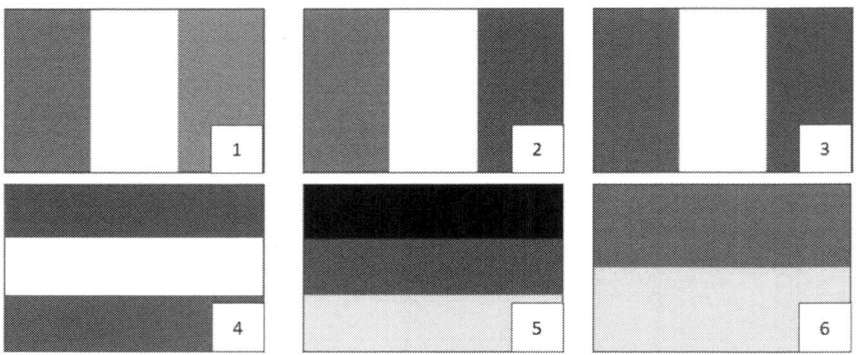

Image: Julia Morris

This example comes from a Geography puzzle where the answers are Ireland, Ukraine and France, so the number code is 1, 6, 3

Example 2: words to code numbers

Here is a biology puzzle based on a text that defines "Ecology", so the code is 9573.

Bacteria 2562	Pesticide 2482	Biochemistry 0838
Hydrolysis 4943	Embryology 9137	Herbicide 9672
Microbiology 4710	Bacteriology 5230	Ecology 9573

Example 3: syllables to numbers

Another biology puzzle where birds must be matched up with their habitat. The answers are Parrot and Robin, so the code is 40, 42, 87, 09

CA 21	PAR 40	RY 79
EAG 23	NA 79	ROT 42
ROB 87	LE 56	IN 09

The answer is a text, but I need a number or short word

Option 1 What is it talking about?: To narrow down a text to one word, base your puzzle on a text that is a definition or description of an item, process or person associated with your subject matter, and the password is the word that is being defined. For example: "A small domesticated carnivorous mammal with soft fur, a short snout, and retractable claws." Codeword: CAT

Option 2 Spot the mistake: Use a topic-based text but include an error that students need to find by using their subject knowledge. The password is either the incorrect word or correction. For example: "Oxygen is a colourless, odourless reactive liquid, the chemical element of atomic number 8." Oxygen is a gas, not a liquid, so the code is either "gas" or 3 (because it has three letters) or the answer is "liquid" or 6.

Options 3 Tables: The students find the word that is being defined or the incorrect word in the table to get a code.

Option 4 Puzzle mix: combine the text puzzle with a number puzzle. When both puzzles are solved, the numbers tell the students which word to use. For example, the number puzzle would give them 5 2 1, so they have to take the 5th line, the second word, first letter.

I am using a digital lock

If you are using digital or imaginary locks, the input options are nearly infinite. Even though it is tempting to use exam-style questions in a digital lock, try to keep the input similar to a real-life lock, e.g. number codes, directions, colours and short passwords. It will help immersion and make it feel more like an escape room and less like an online test. You can still add some additional quiz questions at the beginning of the form to get more educational content into the activity, but the last part of the form should be a traditional passcode.

Whenever students enter answers in an online form, they should be reminded of the story by reading part of the narration or seeing a picture. Depending on the setting you might want to describe the online form as a physical lock: "You have found a mysterious looking box with a four-digit padlock, can envelope five help you to uncover the secret?" (add some pictures of boxes and locks to your form). An online lock is obviously easier to sell as part of a modern setting, e.g. it is the number pad on the sealed door to the secret lab or the password you need to enter to spy on the supervillain's computer system.

CLASSIC ELEMENTS

Hidden Objects

Resources	digital: presentation Physical: paper or props and hiding places around the room
Question	find the object
Answer	any

What does it look like?

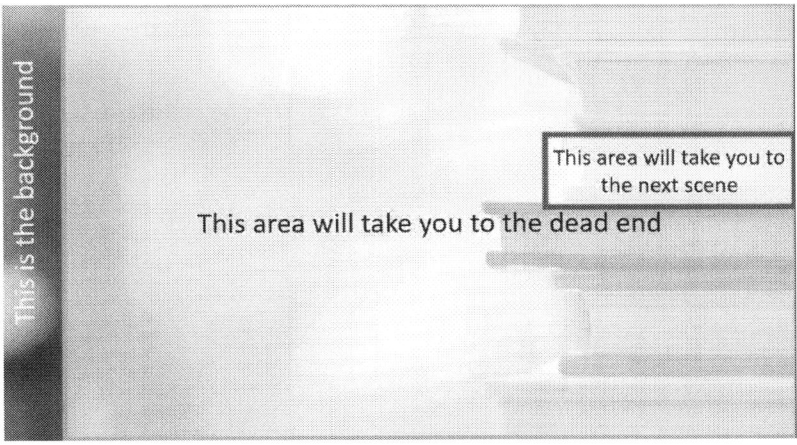
This is the background
This area will take you to the next scene
This area will take you to the dead end

Image: Julia Morris

What is it for?

Finding hidden objects in the room, whether real or digital, is the main element of all escape rooms and also of the classic click-and-point adventure computer games that inspired the first rooms. I feel that an escape room needs to include hidden items, so you should always try to include at least one such activity even though it is not always linked with subject content.

How do I create it?

In a classroom there usually are hundreds of places to hide a piece of paper with a clue: In a book, taped under the table or to the inside of the door handle, hidden behind displays, in cupboards and drawers. If you are playing in teams, it will have the disadvantage that one team can watch another team find items, so you might have to give each team different things to find. One way of doing this is to print team names on the items and making it very clear to the students that they can only pick up their own team items and should not tell other teams where their items are hidden. Another solution to the problem is to have a separate chain of clues for each team. An easy way to start them off is by sticking a hint under the team table or giving it to the team captain. For example, team one would get the clue "Look next to the clock", and when they go there, they find another piece of paper that says "Look under the poster of our last concert" etc. In the meantime, team 2 has to look in completely different places: the first clue might lead them to a specific book, the second one to a drawer etc.

If you are using digital presentations, add pictures of the imaginary locations and get students to "search" the place by clicking on different items or follow clues they have gained in a puzzle. In PowerPoint, Google slides and Google Images you can link items to other slides or websites which means that when the correct item or multiple-choice answer is clicked, it will take the students to the next scene. To do that in PowerPoint or Google slides, right-click the object, select "Link" – "Place in this document" and then chose the slide you want to jump to if the item is clicked. In Genial.ly use the link icon  and then chose the slide to which you want to link.

You can also add an invisible link so that clicking into one area of the picture takes you to another page. For example, if you have a picture of ten books, and you want the link only on the green book, but it is not a separate object. In this case, insert a rectangular shape the same size as the book and position it on top of the background to cover just the one book. Link the rectangle to the next slide, then click "shape format" and change both "shape fill" and "shape outline" to "no colour". Now the rectangle will be invisible, but the link will still be active.

One problem with this method is that the hidden area is easy to discover as the mouse cursor will change into a hand shape when hovering over the field, but there is an easy solution to this. Cover the whole slide with another invisible box that links to a "dead end" slide, but make sure to include a back button which will take them back to the original slide. Make sure the invisible area with the correct link is the top layer on the slide (right-click on it and "move to top"). By having two hidden areas, the mouse cursor will turn into a hand symbol anywhere on the slide, but it will only go the next slide only when the correct place is clicked, otherwise you land on the "dead end". See the example picture above in which all layers have been made visible.

How do the students use it?

Students will need a clear cue when it is time to get up to start searching the room. Just like in real escape rooms, you will need to be very specific about which areas are out of bounds for searches, so put stickers on your personal drawers and lock away your handbag if you want to avoid embarrassing misunderstandings.

Give students clues about where to start searching. It is obviously more fun if you can make the clues more cryptic, and you can include subject knowledge by describing the content of displays or textbooks that hide the secret item.

How could I use it?

- Science: "Find the clues behind the display that describes Newton's greatest discovery."

- Maths: "Stand by the door and take (7x3)-4 steps forwards and 20/4 steps to the left."
- Languages: "Ve a la izquierda y luego sigue recto"

UV Light and Invisible Ink

Resources	digital: Document or presentation paper: worksheet, UV pen and UV torch
Question	find the odd one out, multiple-choice
Answer	letters, numbers, short words

What does it look like?

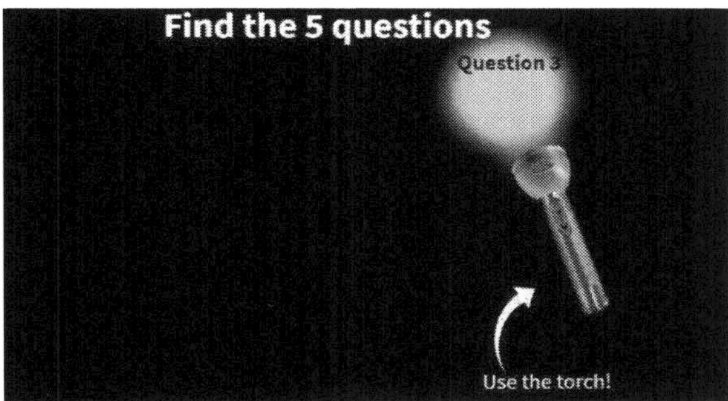

Image: Genial.ly

What is it for?

Everyone loves secret writing and UV torches, and many commercial escape rooms include them. Students need an ultraviolet torch to read a message written in a special ink that is otherwise invisible. Getting the torch and getting the piece of paper with the invisible ink can be two separate activities so that students need to complete both to read the message.

To make the UV writing educational, the invisible words can be the answers to multiple-choice questions (each linked with a code number) or a list of "odd one out" items. You could also write the secret message between the lines or in the margins of a text or a picture. The clue can then be something like: "The first number is in the text where the outcome of the process is described, the second number is in the text in a place where a relevant example is used, and the last number is where the text uses a rhetorical question."

How do I create it?

UV torches are much cheaper than you might expect, and you can buy a pack of UV keyring torches and pens on amazon or eBay for a few pounds. They are also available as UV pens that come with the torch built into the lid. But be careful, they will be popular with the students, and you will need to be careful that they do not keep them as souvenirs. If your escape room takes place in a science lab or kitchen, you could also use the classic method or writing the message with lemon juice. The paper must then be heated up to read the text.

For a digital version, use this method (also see in "Red reveal")

Open a presentation in PowerPoint, Google slides or Genial.ly and insert several text boxes with messages (some of the irrelevant) and spread them all over the screen. Then change the background colour to the same colour as the words, so they are now invisible. Add a circular shape and fill it in white or light purple (to look like a UV light). It looks best if you choose "shape effects" "soft edges" in PowerPoint. Now, right-click and "send to the back". The "light" should now be in a layer between the black background and the black words, so when you move it around the screen, the words will become visible in front of your "beam".

How do the students use it?

Students solve a puzzle to get a code to a box that contains the UV light or a clue of where it is hidden in the classroom (it could be taped under each team's table). They solve a separate puzzle, maybe much later in the sequence of activities, which rewards them with the text with invisible ink. They get some hint that they need to use a torch, e.g. "If only you had something to help you read between the lines..." They shine the torch onto the paper and find the hidden message there.

How could I use it?

- Sports: A picture of a team set up – invisible numbers next to the different positions.
- Science: A picture of an experimental set up with invisible messages next to each stage of the experiment. Students bring the images in the right order to decode the message.
- English Language: Find the place in the text where alliteration was used and note down the invisible codeword next to it.

QR Codes

Resources	digital: Document or presentation +mobile device paper: worksheet + mobile device, black felt-tip pen (for colour-in version)
Question	any
Answer	any medium, can be film, sound, link, text

What does it look like?

What is it for?

A QR code is a unique pattern that can be scanned with a mobile device to show a text or picture, play a sound or link to a website. QR codes can be printed and hidden around the room for students to find. They could be linked to multiple-choice questions: each answer option has a QR code with it so students can scan them to check their answers and get the next clue if they scan the correct one. QR codes can also be used as a part of a hint system: students can scan the code to get some help on how to solve a puzzle.

There is a website where you can print out incomplete QR codes, and students have to colour certain boxes to complete the code.

Unfortunately, at the moment there are only French and German versions of the website available. You can either use the built-in translator of your web browser to find your way around or use the instructions below.

How do I create it?

There are many QR generators online, for example https://www.qr-code-generator.com/ is straightforward to use. At the top, it will give you lots of options of what you want to encode (texts, links, pictures etc.). For some content, you need to create a free account, but you do not need an account to encode weblinks and texts, the two most useful options.

If you want to create a colour-in QR code, go to https://mal-den-code.de/, then select "QR-Code erstellen", and enter a weblink into the top box or a text, e.g. a password, into the bottom box and click "Code zum ausmalen erstellen" to create an incomplete code. The top of the two drop-down boxes asks you how many different numbers will need to be coloured in (either 3, 5 or 10 different ones) and if you want numbers or letters. The last option allows you to enter your own correct answers, separated by a semi-colon. The second drop box changes the size of the area that needs to be coloured. Click "Malvorlage" to download the colouring sheet and click "Lösungsblatt" to print the answer sheet that also tells you at the bottom which numbers need to be coloured in.

How do the students use it?

Most smartphones do not need a QR code app; instead, you can just point the camera on the QR code (do not take a picture) and the link should pop up automatically. Students find the QR codes around the room or as answers on a multiple-choice sheet and scan them to get next hint or passcode.

The colouring-in QR sheet can also be used in combination with multiple-choice questions. The website recommends asking questions like:

What are lions?

A) Mammals – colour all 1s

B) Reptiles – colour all 5s

C) Birds – colour all 9s

For the code to work, pupils need to use black pens, ideally felt-tip, but they do not need to fill the whole box, a big dot can be enough as long as the contrast is big enough. You might need a few spare sheets in case students get it wrong and need to start again.

How could I use it?

- Languages: record spoken questions that are played when the QR is scanned.
- Food: each QR code shows one step in the preparation of a dish, they need to be brought in the right order.
- Maths: take the cross sum of the result the equation below to find the next number to colour.

MATCH UP PUZZLES

Code Wheel

Resources	digital: PowerPoint paper: scissors, cardstock, brass paper fasteners
Question	if this is… then what is…
Answer	words, numbers

What does it look like?

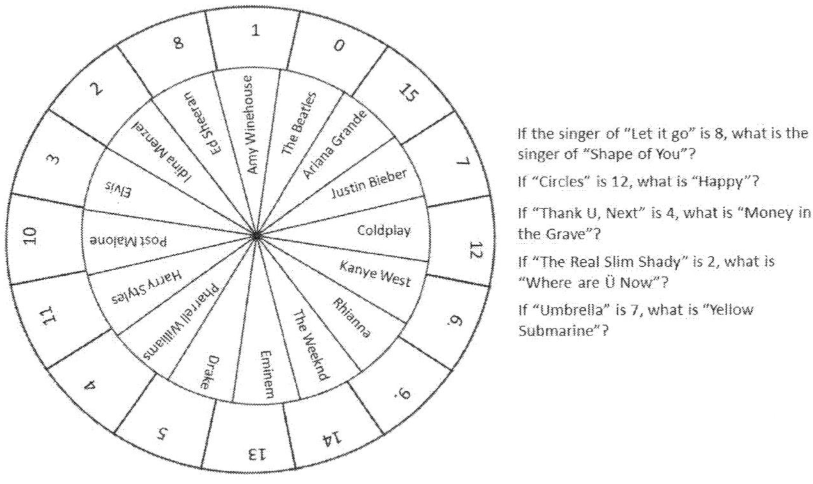

Image: Genial.ly

What is it for?

This is a variation on the Caesar cipher with an educational twist.

For each question, the students need to choose the two correct answer among the 16 options. They line up the answer to the first part of the question with the given number by turning the wheel, then they find the answer to the second part to find the code number next to it. It is made more challenging by the fact that all answers are quite similar (in the example they are all singers) and part of the puzzle is to work out exactly how to apply the "if… then" sentences.

How do I create it?

Create 3-10 questions that follow the pattern: "If the capital of France is 8, what is the capital of Spain?" Ideally, the same numbers should not be used twice in the questions because that might be confusing for the students. You should try the answers out on the wheel as you write them to make sure that each question requires a big enough turn of the wheel (it's more fun!) and that answers are not right next to each other.

For the wheel, you create a larger and a smaller circle in a presentation and they need to be divided into the same number of wedges. As this is hard to create, use my template or search online for an image of "circle with 16 segments" (or however many segments you need). The bigger wheel needs numbers or letters, and the smaller wheel needs short answers in each wedge. Create individual text boxes with the numbers or answers, then rotate them to align them with each wedge. The big wheel and all the numbers need to be selected and grouped, the same with the small wheel and all the answers to make sure the words turn with the wheels. It takes quite long to create the first time, but it is easy to change the answers once created.

If it is used as a paper puzzle, the two wheels need to be cut out individually and then connected with a brass paper fastener (also called a split pin) through the middle of both wheels. This way they can be turned like the hands of a clock to align the answers with different numbers.

If you want to use this as a digital puzzle, use the Genial.ly version which words with lists instead of wheels, or share the

Google/PowerPoint presentation with the students. It does in both, but it is easier to use in PowerPoint as the words are still visible while the wheel is turned.

How do the students use it?

Students need to use their knowledge of the topic to get to a code number. In the example above, the first question is: If the singer of "Let it go" is 8, what is the singer of "Shape of You"? Students need to know or research that the singer of "Let it go" is Idina Menzel and the singer of "Shape of you" is Ed Sheeran. They now turn the wheel to line up Idina Menzel with 8 and can then see that Ed Sheeran is next to number 1, so 1 is the first digit of the passcode.

If the students are using the paper version, they can physically turn the little wheel, but if they are using the digital version, they need to stay in edit mode in the presentation and click into the white area of the little wheel. They can then see a small white "turn" arrow or a "handle" with a circle that they can use to align the answer with the number. It is important that the two centres of the circles stay on top of each other.

How could I use it?

- History: If the date of the start of the second world war lines up with 13, what is the date of England joining the war?
- Physics: If the symbol for iron is 7, what is the symbol for gold?
- Maths: if "33x3" points to F, what does "17x4" point to?
- Literature: if the author of "The Crucible" is 11, what is the author "An Inspector Calls"?

Code String

Resources	digital: Presentation paper: Cardstock, 3 ft string, scissors, (hole punch)
Question	match up
Answer	words, numbers

What does it look like?

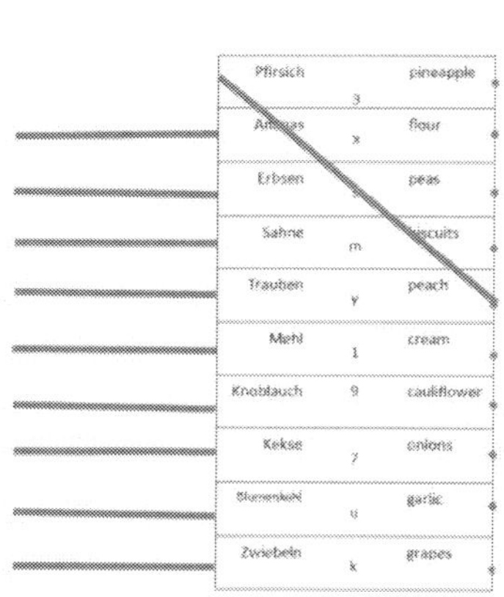

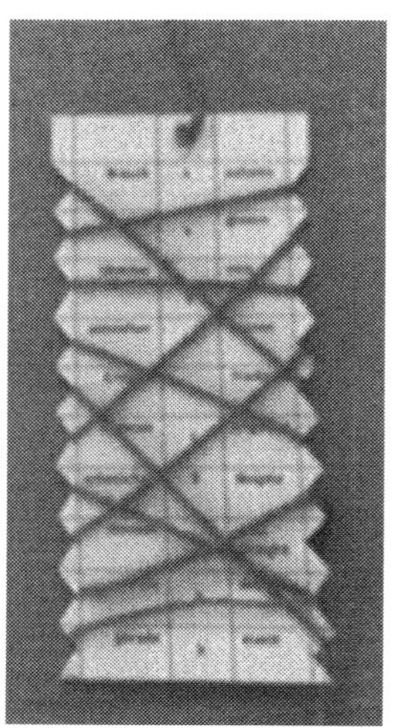

Image: Julia Morris

What is it for?

The students eliminate some of the code numbers/letters in the middle of the card by wrapping a string around the card to connect matching words.

How do I create it?

Create a table with three columns. The left- and right-hand columns contain the matching words, but in a different order on each side. The middle column contains code numbers or letters. When the pairs are connected by a string or by digital lines, one of the letters/numbers in the middle are covered up. The code will consist of all the letters or digits that are still visible in the end. The paper version needs to be printed on cardstock, and a long string needs to be attached through a hole in the centre of the top. Then create grooves next to each word on the left and right to guide the string. A hole punch can make creating it quicker, but you need to make sure the holes are in the middle of the edge of each row.

For the digital version, add the table to a presentation and add a line next to each word on the left to act as the string. To make it more accurate when the students use it, add dots in front of to the answers in the right-hand column to show where the lines should finish.

How do the students use it?

In the digital version, students click the line, then move the endpoint of each line onto the dot next to the matching word. In the paper version, they need to start with the string behind the paper, guide it through the groove on the top left and then through the groove of the matching word. They then go back around the back to the second groove on the left and so on.

In both cases, they need to write down all numbers/letters from the middle that are still clearly visible – they are the passcode.

How could I use it?

- Languages: vocabulary lists
- Geography: Countries and capitals
- Maths: an equation and its solution

Word Strips

Resources	digital: presentation paper: cardstock or worksheet, scissors
Question	unjumble the words
Answer	words

What does it look like?

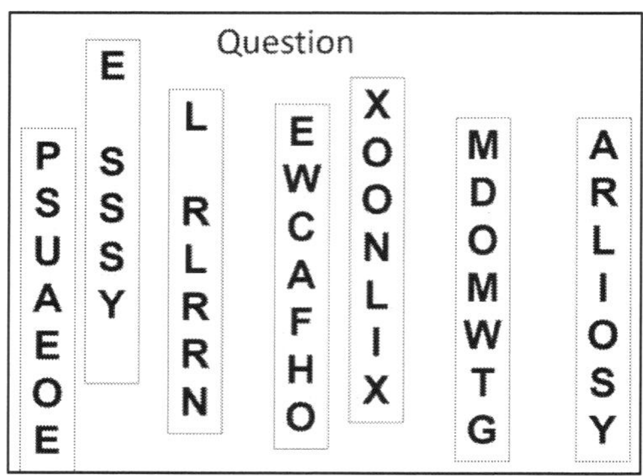

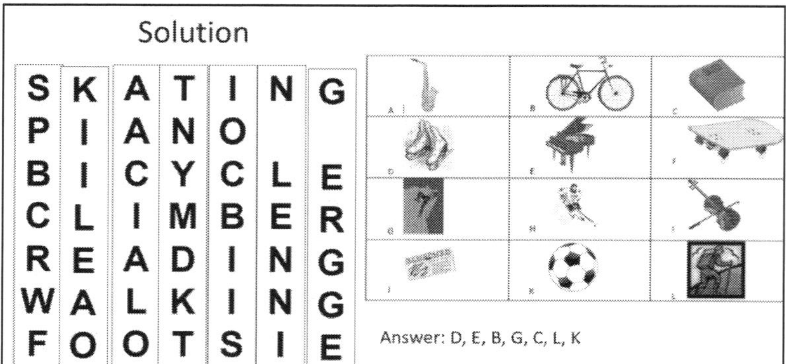

Image: Julia Morris

What is it for?

Students unjumble words in a more tactile way.

How do I create it?

Add a long rectangle on a presentation and duplicate it several times. Line them up next to each other and write the words in, one letter per rectangle, going from left to right. Start with the top word, then move down until you have 5-10 words. Jumble them up on the presentation or cut them out.

To make it more durable, the words could also be written on ice lolly sticks or gardening labels instead of paper strips.

To turn the words into a code, link it with a table (see "How do I make the code fit my lock).

How do the students use it?

There are two parts to this task. First, they unjumble the words. They really only need to recognise one of the words and the others will fall into place, except if there are two identical letters in the word, in that case, another letter on the same strip can help with finding the right order. The task is easier if one of the words contains less common letters like x or z and so stands out. To add an extra challenge, the task could be designed so that the strips also need to be moved upwards and downwards with some letters not being used or forming shorter words.

The second part is to match up the words with the pictures or definitions in a table to turn them into a code.

How could I use it?

- Maths: equations and answers written as words
- P.E.: parts of the body, sports moves
- Geography: outlines/flags of countries

Jigsaw Puzzles and Tarsias

Resources	digital: presentation paper: worksheet, scissors
Question	match up the words or reconstruct the text
Answer	short words or numbers

What does it look like?

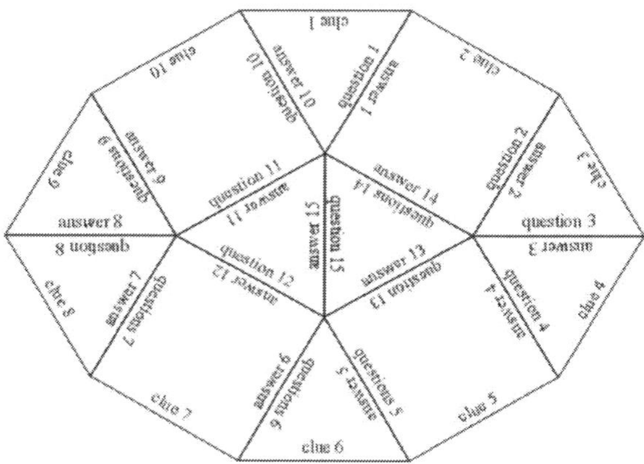

Image: Julia Morris

What is it for?

A jigsaw puzzle can consist of a picture or a text. If all pieces have the same shape, students will need to use their knowledge of the content to assemble it.

A tarsia is a jigsaw puzzle that consists of triangles, each with a word or number on the edge that need to be placed next to a matching word/equation.

How do I create it?

To create a digital picture jigsaw, you will need a free account for jigsawplanet.com, and you are then able to upload any picture, including a screenshot of a text. A disadvantage is that the students can click the "image" button at the bottom to see a preview of the picture which makes it relatively easy, but most of my students did not discover this feature. https://im-a-puzzle.com/ is a similar site that offers the option to hide the preview, but only for premium subscribers.

To create a paper tarsia puzzle, you can download a free tarsia generator from www.mmlsoft.com/index.php/products/tarsia , which gives you lots of different options for size and shape. I recommend using an "extended jigsaw", it has extra words or numbers on the outside that can form the passcode. The tarsia generator was designed for maths tasks, so if you are using text questions and answers, change the input style to "text", before you start typing; otherwise, it will automatically remove all spaces between words.

If you cannot use the software, use the PowerPoint template: Change all questions and answers on slide 1 (change them in pairs, so you know which ones go together). The words called "clue" on the template should not have a matching partner and will end up on the edge of the completed jigsaw. Change the clue words so that the first letters spell out a code.

You can also simply cut up a printed picture or text with scissors. It is best to use straight lines, so the students need to go by the content of the image and cannot just use the shape of the pieces to assemble it. If using a text, you can create a table in word, paste your text into the cells, then highlight it and go into the layout tab. You can now define the size of the cells so all puzzle pieces will be the same size. Make sure to tell the students how many pieces per row and column finished puzzle needs to be.

Text-based jigsaw puzzles come in three difficulty levels. The easiest level is if each puzzle piece ends in the middle of a word. For the medium level, end each piece in the middle of a sentence. This can still be very challenging if the text is in a foreign language or describes a complex process that the students have not come across before. The most difficult are jigsaw pieces that contain a full sentence each. To solve it, students will need to know the chronological order of events or understand the steps in a process that is being described.

For paper jigsaw puzzles I recommend cutting the pieces for the students as younger students can take quite a long time to do cut it themselves, and it also saves you having to generate a jumbled-up version to print.

How do the students use it?

Students assemble the jigsaw puzzle/tarsia. If they are working on a tarsia puzzle, they take the first letters of all words that are on the outside of the shape to get a codeword.

If using a jigsaw puzzle, the codeword/number could be written in large letters across the picture so it can only be read if most of the puzzle is put together. Alternatively, pieces can be numbered on the front or back of the pieces, and students get a clue like "take the third one in the second row, the fifth one in the sixth row etc."

How could I use it?

Tarsias - any short question and answer:

- Maths: equations and answers
- Languages: words that mean the opposite
- History: event and date

Other jigsaws:

- Art: paintings by different artists
- English: a poem, scene from a play
- Science: the steps in an experiment

Crosswords

Resources	digital: online paper: worksheet
Question	what does the clue describe
Answer	words

What does it look like?

Example 1: Normal crossword, with highlighted letters

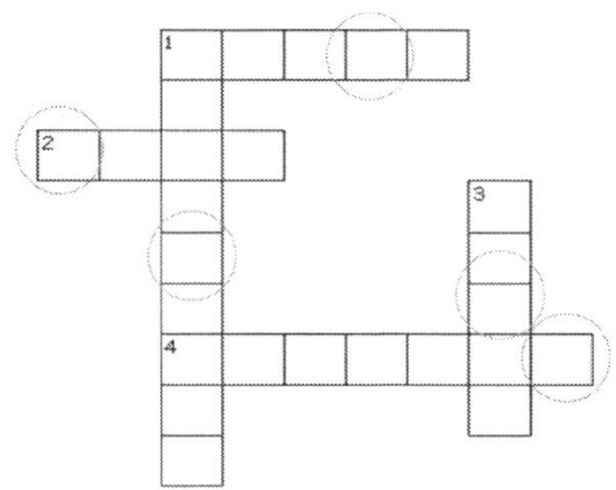

What is it in German?

Across
1. cat
2. dog
4. hamster

Down
1. rabbit
3. bird

Example 2: Crossword gap fill text

Housing stress describes a situation where the – <u>3 down</u> - of housing is high relative to household - <u>4 across</u>- . It may also be used to describe inadequate housing for a proportion of the – <u>1 down -</u> .

Example 3: Reverse crossword

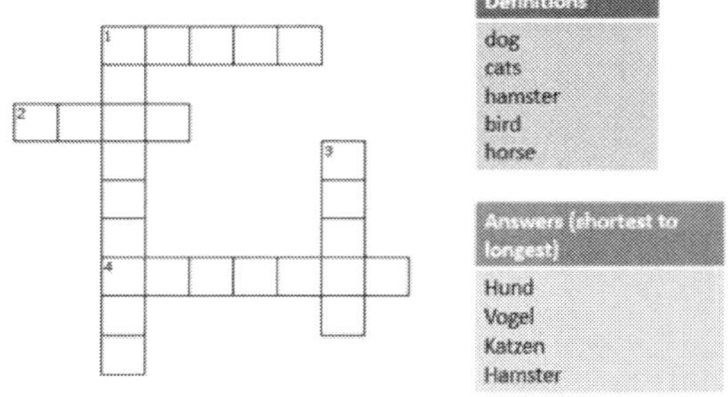

Definitions
dog
cats
hamster
bird
horse
Answers (shortest to longest)
Hund
Vogel
Katzen
Hamster

Across:

1. ____________________
2. ____________________
4. ____________________

Down:

1. ____________________
3. ____________________

Example 4: Picture crossword

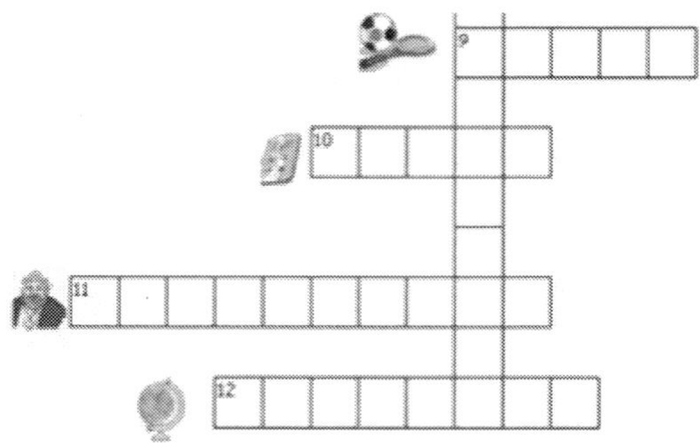

What is it for?

In the classical version, players find answers for definitions fill them into the correct boxes, but there are many variations on the activity (see examples). To get code letters, circle certain boxes. In the end, the letters need to be unjumbled to form a word. The advantage is that your list of words can be as long or short as you want, and the students can see straight away if their answers are correct because otherwise it will not fit.

How do I create it?

To create a classic paper crossword, use "criss cross" on http://puzzlemaker.discoveryeducation.com/. Enter the answer word followed by a space and the definition. Then take a screenshot and add it to document. I recommend printing it and filling it in by hand to decide on the best boxes to highlight for your code– they need to contain the right letters to form a codeword – to make it easier to create (and harder to guess), you could use random letters that then need to be entered into a form or picked out from a list to open the lock. Once you have chosen the correct boxes, add the screenshot to a PowerPoint presentation. Add circle shapes to some of the boxes (change "shape fill" to "no fill").

To create the other variations on crossword puzzles, you can still use the puzzlemaker website but change the list of clues into a different format, like a gap fill text.

The easiest way of making a picture-based crossword is by showing a list of pictures and replacing the clues with "Down 1: Picture 5" etc. If you want to put the images into the crossword, add a screenshot of the crossword puzzle to PowerPoint and then drag the pictures next to each line of boxes.

In a reverse crossword, the students get the answers but have to work out the definitions. This works best work with straight forward pairs or words, e.g. English word and translation in a foreign language or name of animal and name of its young

In this version, the letters for the code need to come from the clue words. Give students the crossword but with empty clues and indicate certain letters like this:

Down:

1. _____________ (3rd letter)
2. _____________ (first letter)

Across:

3._______________ (last letter)

It is helpful to give them a list of all the words that go into the crossword. The students now work out where the words go in the crossword, based on their length alone. Then they fill the definition in the correct place and take the 3rd letter etc. to unjumble them to a password.

For a fully digital version, use www.learningapps.org to create a crossword app. Add the code into the feedback box, so students only get it if they complete the whole crossword.

How do the students use it?

Students use the clues to fill in the words. Then take all letters in circled boxes to unjumble them to form a word or find them in a table.

How could I use it?

- Business: A definition of an economic term (as in Example 3)
- English language: definition are example sentences, answers are names of figurative speech like alliteration, hyperbole etc.
- Religious Studies: Picture crossword with religious symbols as the hints.

Red Reveal

Resources	digital: Presentation paper: colour copy of worksheet, red transparent sheet, cardstock
Question	multiple-choice
Answer	words, numbers

What does it look like?

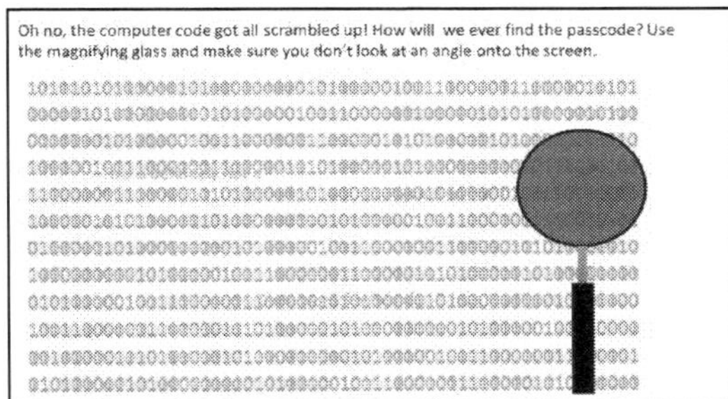

Image: Julia Morris

What is it for?

A classic of kids' detective games: the answers are hidden behind a coloured pattern and are only revealed when a piece of red-tinted transparent paper is laid on top.

How do I create it?

For both the digital and the paper version, you need to create a pattern in certain colours that will hide your words. The S'cape website has a template to create a jumbled-up text in the right colours:
http://scape.enepe.fr/ressources/polychromacryptographe/. Click the gear icon to change the text and use the highlighter icon to see

the solution. The settings page is in French, but if you play with the options, you can quickly see what each one does. Simply put the text you want to hide in the first text box. You can then take a screenshot and insert it into a presentation.

You can also create a jumbled text yourself by opening a PowerPoint or Google presentation and write a whole screen full of random numbers or letters, in a yellow font. Copy and paste the text into a new text box, change the colour to a reddish-pink font and add another few random characters to the beginning and place both texts on top of each other. The letters should not exactly cover each other now but create an unreadable mess. Repeat to get another layer of red text. In a light blue font, write the answers in different text boxes and place them randomly across the background text. They should be impossible to read, otherwise, change the colours of the texts to a lighter blue and lighter red until you cannot read it anymore.

For the paper version:

Print the slide in colour. Print a red circle on a sheet of transparent foil, e.g. a laminating sheet. Then print out a magnifying glass or a pair of glasses onto cardstock and insert the red sheet as the lens.

For the digital version:

Take a screenshot and insert it into a new presentation that is given to the students (so they cannot just move the red text away).

Insert a circular shape. Change the fill colour to bright red and give it a black outline. In the "shape fill" menu, click on "more fill colours" and change the transparency to 20% or less. Now, the answers should become visible if the red circle is moved across the text, and you look at the screen from straight on. To make it look better, add the picture of a handle to your lens to make it look like a magnifying glass and group them.

The digital version saves you expensive colour copying, but it only works if the students look at the screen from a very straight angle, which is not always easy to find. To avoid this problem, you can cheat a bit and put the magnifying glass on a layer between the jumbled background and the words (see UV light).

The Genial.ly link in the link collection includes several variations on the activity, for example "find the words in the rainbow".

How do the students use it?

The students move the red lens across the jumbled text to discover the hidden words. Add different numbers to the secret words to form a code.

- Science: Find the four names of noble gases and note down the numbers next to them. Ignore all the other elements.
- Food: discover the five food items on the page. What do they have in common?
- History: Find the names of 4 famous explorers. Research the year they were born in and add up all the years to find the 4-digit code.

Transparency

Resources	digital: Presentation paper: at least three sheets of transparency foil, permanent marker pen
Question	category
Answer	words

What does it look like?

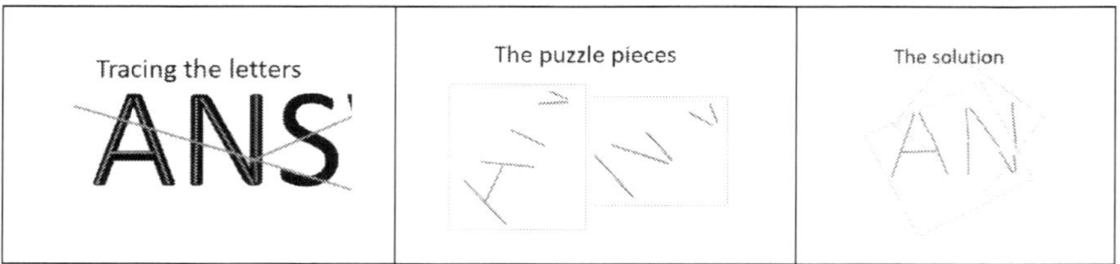

What is it for?

This is a more physical puzzle where several transparent sheets need to be placed on top of each and rotated until they line up to form letters.

How do I create it?

Paper Version:

Write or print your answer words or sentence on a regular piece of paper in big letters. Split each letter into several sections by drawing a line across them.

Now lay the first transparent sheet on top of the writing. Trace a few sections of each letter onto the foil. Ideally, it should not be possible to guess which letter they will form. Do the same with the other foils so that each has a part of each letter on it and the whole text will only become legible if the foils are all placed in the right position. To make it more challenging, turn the sheets to random angles when tracing so that the pile of sheets will not have straight edges when they form the letters.

Digital Version:

You can create it in a similar way to the paper version. Type the words and they "trace" parts of each letter by inserting straight lines. When you have traced the whole word, click on some of the lines while holding down "ctrl". Then right-click and group them. Move them out of the way and do the same for the next lot of lines. Again, it will be more challenging to puzzle together again if they cut up letters are at random angles. For that, click the group of lines, and turn them using the turning arrow or dot at to top. To make sure student cannot easily see what the original orientation was, take screenshots of each group after you have rotated them and add all the screenshots to the presentation that the students will use.

How do the students use it?

Students rotate the lines until they form words. In a physical game, it is best if they find all the pieces in different places at different times. For the digital activity, they need to use the presentation in edit mode to be able to rotate the pieces.

How could I use it?

- R.E.: The name of a holy place that can be found on a poster in the room. The next hint is hidden behind the poster.
- Languages: The next code in Spanish
- Technology: The outline of a tool. The tool can be found in the room, and the next code is taped to the underside.

Picture or Word Additions

Resources	digital: Document or presentation paper: worksheet
Question	word plus word
Answer	pictures, words or short phrases

What does it look like?

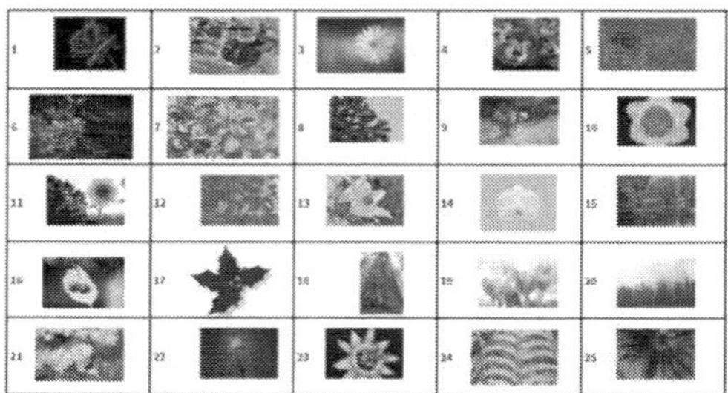

Palm Tree minus Tulip
Plus Beech Tree
minus Orchid
Plus Hazel
Minus Daffodil
Minus Snowdrop
What flower?

Image: Genial.ly

What is it for?

Use pictures in an unusual way: add or subtract them to get to the next clue.

How do I create it?

Create a grid and fill each cell with a picture or word. Each cell also needs a number, either in order or randomly.

Then write 4-10 word equations like above, adding or subtracting the numbers in the boxes. Make sure the solution to the equation can be found in the grid.

It could be one long equation like in the example above so that students will end up with one number. It could also be several individual equations that will give students several numbers or words. Hints for the equations can be much longer than in the example above:

(A tree commonly found in tropical climates, valued for its large nuts) minus (a spring-blooming perennial associated with the Netherlands)

How do the students use it?

Students read the first equation, e.g. "Palm Tree minus Tulip". They use their subject knowledge to find the correct pictures in the grid, in this case 25 (Palm) and 19 (Tulip) and can now solve the equation: 25-19= 6 (Clematis).

In a digital version, you can give one equation at a time and add an invisible area to the correct answer. When clicked, it will take the students to the next equations until they get to the last slide that reveals the code.

How could I use it?

- Science: Periodic table
- Music: musical instruments
- Geography: parts of a river system

Category Maze

Resources	digital: Document or presentation paper: worksheet
Question	1-4 categories
Answer	a list of short phrases, numbers, pictures

What does it look like?

Red here

Blue start here

1 Kidnapped	2 A School for Scandal	3 The Mayor of Casterbridge	4 Romeo and Juliet	5 Dracula
6 Goblet of Fire	7 Animal Farm	8 Richard III	9 Macbeth	10 The Trial
11 Sorcerer's Stone	12 Order of the Phoenix	13 Tempest	14 Brave New World	15 Woyzeck
16 The Pickwick Papers	17 Chamber of Secrets	18 Hamlet	19 Anthony and Cleopatra	20 War and Peace
21 Deathly Hallows	22 Prisoner of Azkaban	23 Mockingjay	24 Othello	25 Tartuffe
26 To Kill a Mockingbird	27 The Lion, the Witch and the Wardrobe	28 The Little Prince	29 Midsummer Night's Dream	30 She Stoops to Conquer

Image: Julia Morris

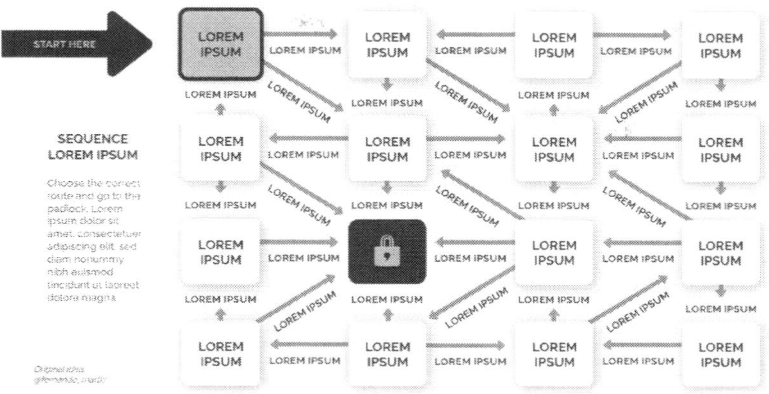

Template by Genial.ly, original idea @fernando_mati7

What is it for?

This puzzle asks students to decide if a word, number or phrase falls into a certain category. Part of the task can be to find out what the categories themselves are. This requires students to recognise similarities or recall facts that connect the words.

In the first example picture, students find 30 book titles, and they need to pick out all Harry Potter titles for the blue path and Shakespeare plays for the red.

How do I create it?

You need to create a grid at least 4x4, e.g. by inserting a table into a document. Decide on a starting place for each category, each on a different side of the grid. Highlight the starting place by placing an arrow or adding an extra "start here" box on the side. It is easier if the category is given, harder if the students need to find it out themselves. The box next to the starting point needs to contain the first correct answer, the next solution should be in an adjacent box so all correct answers will form a path. The last correct answer should be at the edge of the grid. All other boxes need to contain distractors. These are important because the more similar they are to the possible answers, the more the students will have to think about the options and not just guess. Each box also needs to contain a number or a letter.

How do the students use it?

Students need to find the path(s) of answers for each category and then take all the numbers in the correct boxes to form the passcode. In the example above it would be 61112172221 for blue and 4981318192429 for red. To get a shorter code they could be added up, so blue would be 89 and red 124. If you are using letters that form a word instead of numbers, it will allow students to spot mistakes before trying to input the code, but it would also allow for guessing.

How could I use it?

- Art: parts of a camera vs parts of a computer
- P.E.: muscle groups
- History: Events in different years – the events also must be found in the right chronological order

Cards

Resources	digital: Document or presentation paper: worksheet, scissors (optional)
Question	find all words from a category
Answer	choice of short phrases, numbers, pictures

What does it look like?

1. Remove all Australian animals.
2. Take the smallest bird that cannot fly, followed by the largest land animal.
3. Take every third mammal that hasn't been used
4. First 3 reptiles backwards.
5. Rest of the reptiles backwards, but only if they can swim.
6. Take all remaining birds and reptiles interspersed evenly, starting with birds.

Image: Julia Morris

What is it for?

This activity is a variation on a logic grid puzzle, with pictures or cards instead of a table. Just like in a logic puzzle, players are given a list of rules to follow that help them to cross out cards or tell them in which order to "deal" them. This game is based on a game by Dani Siller from https://www.escapethispodcast.com/ and was originally played with a deck of playing cards, but it has been given a more educational spin here by using subject-specific words. Like in the original game, each card is labelled with a letter. When the rules are followed, the letters are brought in the right order and spell out a hint or a password. It works best if the hidden message is quite long and cannot easily be guessed.

How do I create it?

Your words should fall into 2-5 different categories to be able to write clear rules. Create your desired number of cards, depending on the length of your message. You can just draw squares on a presentation and duplicate them, and then share them electronically, print them as a worksheet or cut them out. If you want to make it more tactile, you could use a real deck of cards and write or stick extra words or pictures on them.

Mix up the cards and get students to move them around to sort them by category and put them into the right order. They must be in a set order from left to right, so the first task should be "Sort the cards into categories, then sort them from smallest to largest/newest to oldest etc."

If you are using Google and PowerPoint, students will need to stay in edit mode to be able to move objects around the screen, and in Genial.ly the "drag items" option needs to be selected in settings. In Genial.ly, you can also create a more complicated version where students must "turn" each card around to see what is written on it. To make it, add a cover to each card that looks like the back of the card, then add an animation to the cover, and select "hover mouse" -

"hide". If students now move their mouse over the card, the cover will disappear, and the front of the card with the word will become visible for a short time.

How do the students use it?

Students bring the cards in the specified order if they are cut out. Then they follow the instructions and discard some cards and find the right order for the others and note down the letters on a piece of paper to decode the message.

How could I use it?

- Science: Animals and plants sorted by biomes
- English: Words sorted by word class, by alphabet, numbers of syllables, order in which they appear in a poem
- Design and Technology: furniture or outfits sorted by style, age or material

Spot the Difference

Resources	digital: Document or presentation paper: worksheet
Question	what is the difference/what is the same?
Answer	pictures/words

What does it look like?

Image: Julia Morris

What is it for?

Every child knows "Spot the difference" puzzles, but here it has been taken up a notch by having four instead of two pictures to compare. Students need to find the images that are either in all four boxes or the object that is not in all of the boxes. They can then take the associated numbers and add them up to find a passcode.

There are two different ways of given this fun puzzle an educational element. Option 1 is to play in pairs, with each player looking at only two of the four pictures which they have to describe to each other to work out together, what items are missing. This way, they need to know the name of the people or objects to be able to describe them effectively.

Option 2 is to have matching but not identical items that belong to one group, e.g. box one has a face of a politician, box 2 the flag of their country, box 3 a date and box 4 the name of the main event with which they are associated. Once students have found all four elements of each group, they can cross them out. Whichever item is left at the end gives them code number.

How do I create it?

Insert a table in a presentation or document. Make all boxes the same size by going into the layout options and specifying the height and width. Add pictures or words, ideally in different sizes, directions and fonts to make it harder to spot the similarities and add a list of all possible items or groups and give each a code number.

How do the students use it?

Students find between 1-5 items that are the only ones that (do not) appear in all boxes. Once they have found them, they take the associated numbers and add them up to get the code.

How could I use it?

- Maths: Different equations that add up to the same result
- Geography: sights or facts associated with the same country
- Art: Different works by the same artist

Dot to Dot

Resources	paper: presentation to create, worksheet
Question	words, numbers, sentences
Answer	numbers, words,

What does it look like?

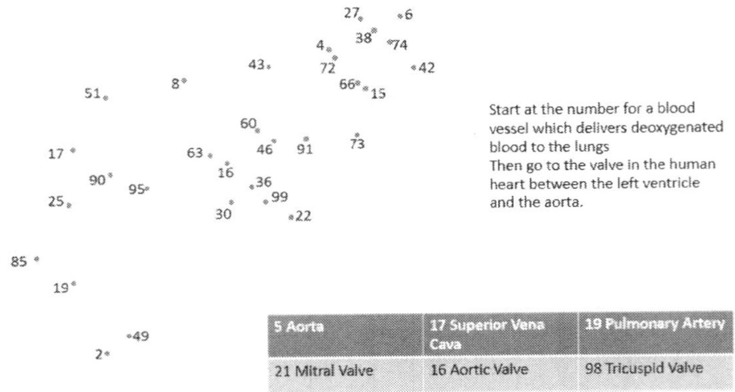
Start at the number for a blood vessel which delivers deoxygenated blood to the lungs
Then go to the valve in the human heart between the left ventricle and the aorta.

5 Aorta	17 Superior Vena Cava	19 Pulmonary Artery
21 Mitral Valve	16 Aortic Valve	98 Tricuspid Valve

Image: Julia Morris

What is it for?

Children of every age love dot to dot, especially if it is not obvious from the beginning what the picture is. In regular dot to do activities, you connect the dots with straight lines starting from one, then two etc., but for an educational twist, the numbers here are not in the right order, and there are lots of numbers that are not going to be used at all. With the help of a table, like in the example above, any topic can be the basis of a dot to dot.

In this example, students need to recall the parts of the heart. Each word relates to a (random) number in the table. The text then tells them where to start their dot to dot, in this case “the blood vessel that delivers..." (number 19). The next hint describes the aortic valve, so the first line goes from 19 to 16.

How do I create it?

Making your own dot to dot can take some time. http://www.picturedots.com/ is a useful website for turning pictures into dots. It only generates traditional dot to dot with numbers in the right order, but you could take a screenshot, add it to a presentation and cover all numbers with text boxes with your choice of random numbers.

You can also create your own picture in a PowerPoint/Google presentation. Choose a simple, clear picture of the object you want to turn into dot to dot, ideally a clipart image. Then create a very small filled-in circle by inserting a shape. Copy and paste the circle lots of times and distribute them along the outline of your picture. Remove the image to see if the dots resemble the shape that you are after, then insert text boxes with random numbers or letters or even short words next to each dot. Make sure you do not use the same number twice! I would recommend NOT to include numbers 1-10 because students are so primed to do dot to dots in the right order, they will automatically try to start at one and are likely to overlook any other instructions or hints.

Now there are two options: if your questions have numbers as the answer, e.g. maths problems or translating numbers from a foreign language, you can just write a list of your hints. E.g. Start at 6x3, then 5x9, 3x2...

If your answers are longer, add a table that includes all the numbers that will be needed as well as some decoy ones and add a word/sentence to each number. Then write your hints that will lead students to the correct cell, like in the example above.

Once you have your numbers and have written a table with associated words and your instructions, create more dots and spread all over the picture to disguise the shape. Make sure you do not use any numbers twice by mistake.

How do the students use it?

Students follow the hints to connect the dots. The lines could spell out a word or number or show the picture of an object that has to be found in the classroom or whose name is the codeword. If you are creating a digital resource, students must click the correct word/picture of the object to get to the next activity.

How could I use it?

- Languages: dix, treize, vingt-neuf...
- Physics: Which word describes force x distance
- Media Studies: Find the word for the camera angle that is most used in filming two people talking.

Snotes

Resources	digital: Presentation and snotes.com paper: worksheet
Question	short sentence
Answer	words

What does it look like?

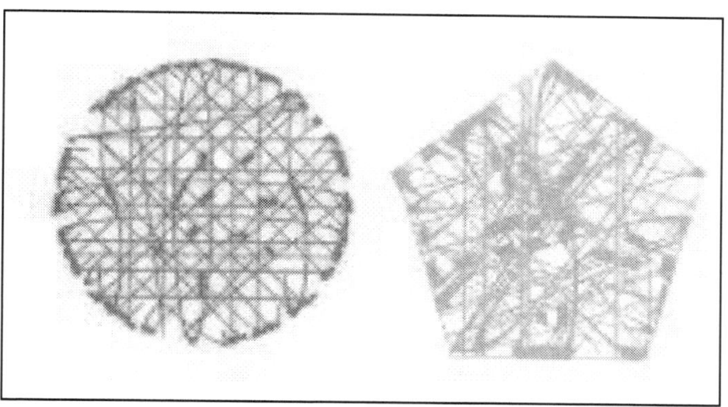

Image: snotes.com

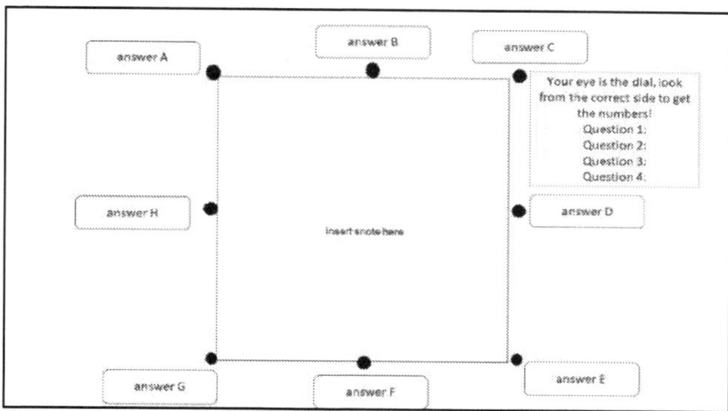

What is it for?

On www.snotes.com you can create hidden message consisting of a list of words (not more than 20 characters). It looks like a confusing pattern until you look at it from a low angle from the side and suddenly, words will appear.

How a snote works: https://youtu.be/965flcMtRE0

How do I create it?

To create a worksheet to use with your snote, use the template above and insert your snote or create your own on a presentation by putting text boxes with around the snote. They will indicate from which way to look.

To create the snote go to the website. If you do not want to sign up for a free account, simply use the snote created during the tutorial, but you will need a free account if you want to download it and not just screenshot it and to create snotes with more than four words. You could also take advantage of the 48h of free teacher access that allows you to create a special escape room design card – you can find it in the "educator" section.

How do the students use it?

There are different ways of using this with subject content.

1. The words hidden in the snote all have something in common, and the common denominator is the codeword, e.g. verbs or minerals
2. Ask a question with several possible answers, but only one of the words in the snotes fits the question, e.g. What is a large town in South Africa? Which of these people did not live in the 20th century? The odd one out is the password.
3. The words could form a sentence or quote and need to be brought in the right order. The first letters then form the codeword. E.g. It was the best of times = I W T B O T.
4. To use the worksheet, you need several questions that have similar answers. The answers are written on different sides of

the snote, like in the template. The words in the snote need to be numbers that will form a passcode. To find out which of the numbers are needed and in which order, the students need to answer the questions and then look from the correct direction sideways onto the snote and find the number. For example, answer box A says, "hard drive" answer B says "printer" and answer C says "monitor". The first question is "What part of a computer is an output device that displays information in pictorial form"? The students then look onto the snote from the side that says "monitor" and see the number 6 hidden in the picture. They now know that this is the first number of the passcode.

Colour Changer

Resources	digital: spreadsheet
Question	sentences
Answer	exact words or numbers

What does it look like?

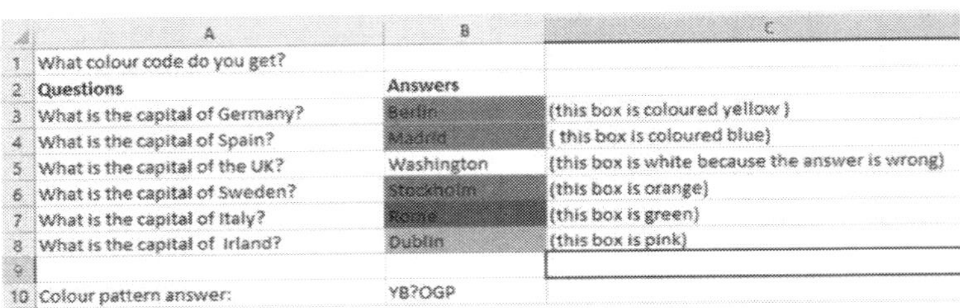

	A	B	C
1	What colour code do you get?		
2	**Questions**	**Answers**	
3	What is the capital of Germany?	Berlin	(this box is coloured yellow)
4	What is the capital of Spain?	Madrid	(this box is coloured blue)
5	What is the capital of the UK?	Washington	(this box is white because the answer is wrong)
6	What is the capital of Sweden?	Stockholm	(this box is orange)
7	What is the capital of Italy?	Rome	(this box is green)
8	What is the capital of Irland?	Dublin	(this box is pink)
9			
10	Colour pattern answer:	YB?OGP	

What is it for?

Students enter an exact answer into a spreadsheet which gives them a colour code if it is correct.

How do I create it?

You need to create a spreadsheet with a column of questions and an answer column in which each cell has different "conditional formatting" assigned to it. The cell will then change colour if the correct answer is put in and enter is pressed or the next box is selected.

In Excel:

1. Enter the headings "Questions" and "Answers" to make clear where students need to type.
2. Enter a list of questions in the first column.
3. Click on the first answer box. In the "Home" tab, choose "Conditional formatting".
4. Click "New rule".

5. Select the rule type "Format only cells that contain".
6. In the drop-down boxes, change "Cell Value" to "Specific text" if the answer is a word. If the answer is a number, skip this step.
7. The second drop-down box should be "containing".
8. In the text box, enter the answer. It is not case sensitive.
9. Click "format" at the bottom.
10. Choose the colour. Each box should turn a different colour. From experience, I would recommend avoiding red, at least for the first box, as it can easily be interpreted as "the wrong answer".
11. Click "ok" and try it out, but make sure to delete all answer before sharing the spreadsheet with the students.

In Google Sheets:

1. Enter the headings "Questions" and "Answers" to make clear where students need to type.
2. Enter a list of questions in the first column.
3. Click the first answer box. In the "Format" menu, chose "conditional formatting".
4. Change the drop-down menu "Format cells if…" to "Text is exactly".
5. In the box "Value or formula", insert your answer.
6. In the menu "Formatting Style", click the paint pot.
7. Choose the colour. Each box should turn a different colour. From experience, I would recommend avoiding red, at least for the first box, as it can easily be interpreted as "wrong answer".
8. Click "ok" and try it out, but make sure to delete all answer before sharing the spreadsheet with the students.

You could add links to helpful websites next to each question to encourage research.

How do the students use it?

Students open the spreadsheet and insert the answers. They then take the colours to open a colour lock or take the colours' first letters to open a letter lock.

How could I use it?

- R.E.: To the nearest million, how many Hindus are there in the world? Which country has the largest Hindu population? What is the Hindu name of the "Creator"?
- English: What literary device is being used here "All amazing alligators"? What is used here "Her skin was white as snow"?
- Music: Listen to the track in the link and name the main instrument/composer/style.

Directional Maze

Resources	digital: spreadsheet and document or worksheet
Question	sentences
Answer	exact words or numbers

What does it look like?

	A	B	C	D	E	F	G
1	Follow the lines through the maze				The Maze		
2	Questions	Answers		Start here	4577	8562	4562
3	What is the capital of Germany?	[illegible]		6744	7902	6820	2820
4	What is the capital of Spain?	[illegible]		7283	1296	1647	8647
5	What is the capital of the UK?	[illegible]		7742	4762	9693	5693
6	What is the capital of Sweden?	[illegible]					
7	What is the capital of Italy?	[illegible]					
8				Answer here: 5693			

What is it for?

This is a variation on the colour changer spreadsheet, just in this case the students get hints on directions (vertical, horizontal, diagonal left/right) that will guide them through a simple maze.

How do I create it?

In Excel (does not work in Google Sheets):

It is created the same way as the colour changer above, but in step 10, choose a "pattern style" instead of a colour.

You then need to create a "maze", which could be a simple 4x4 grid in which each box contains a different code number/word/picture. It is easiest to create the maze as a table in a document and then print it as a worksheet or copy it into the spreadsheet.

As there is no clear distinction between left and right, make sure it is obvious which way to go, e.g. only use horizontal stripes when the box is on the edge of the grid.

How do the students use it?

Students open the spreadsheet and insert the answers. They then take the directions indicated by the stripes in the cells to "move" through the maze to end up on the correct code to open the next lock. In the example above, after they put in the correct answers, they start in the start box, then go to 7902 because the stripes go diagonally right. Then they go to the box 7283 because the stripes point diagonally left. From here they go to 1296 as indicated by the vertical stripes (there is no option to go left so it must be right) etc.

How could I use it?

- R.E.: To the nearest million, how many Hindus are there in the world? Which country has the largest Hindu population? What is the Hindu name of the "Creator"?
- English: What literary device is being used here "All amazing alligators"? What is used here "Her skin was white as snow"?
- Music: Listen to the track in the link and name the main instrument/composer/style.

Number Changer

Resources	digital: spreadsheet
Question	sentences
Answer	exact numbers

What does it look like?

	A	B	C	D	E
1					
2	**Answer all questions in number, you will then get a code**				
3	**question**	**Answer**	**Code number**		
4	Periodic number of iron	26	3		
5	Periodic number of silver	47	13		
6	Periodic number of gold	79	=IF(B6=79,8,0)		
7			IF(logical_test, [value_if_true], [value_if_false])		
8					
9					
10	**Passcode**				

What is it for?

This is a variation on the colour changer, but it will turn number answers into code numbers. See "How could I use it" for ideas how to use even if you teach a subject other than maths.

How do I create it?

The activity does not use conditional formatting, but instead a formula. It works in Excel and Google Sheets.

In the cell where you want your code to appear, type something like =IF (B6=79, 8, 0).

The equal sign and "IF" (in capital letters) indicate that it is a formula. The first information inside the brackets needs to be the letter and number of the cell where the student will put the answer (in this case B6,) followed by another equal sign and the correct answer (here 79). The next two number show what will be displayed if the answer is correct (here 8) and what is the answer is wrong (here 0).

How do the students use it?

Students open the spreadsheet and enter the answers in the form of a number in the answer column and then take all numbers from the "code number" column to get the passcode.

Careful: if your students are experts in using spreadsheets, they can discover the answer by double-clicking the answer box.

How could I use it?

To generate number answers:

- On what page of the textbook can you find the answer to the following question…?
- How many letters does the answer to the following question have…?
- On the following list of answers, which number answers the question…? (numbers associated with solutions do not need to be in order, they could be random 3-digit codes.)
- For shorter words: replace A with 1, B with 2 etc.

TEXT-BASED PUZZLES

Caesar Cipher

Resources	digital: presentation (PowerPoint works better than Google Slides) paper: scissors, cardstock, brass paper fasteners
Question	encrypted text
Answer	text

What does it look like?

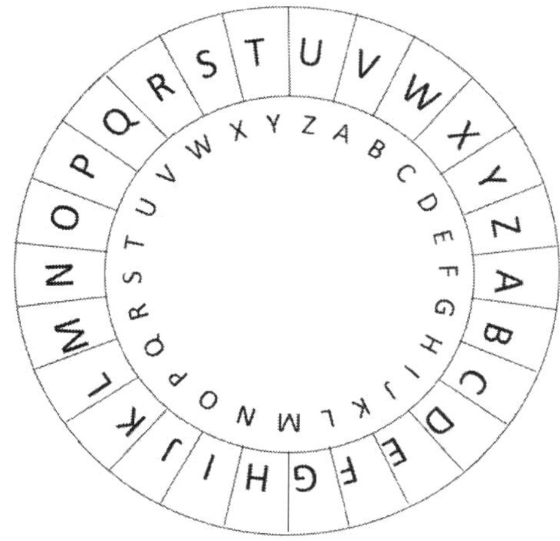

Image: Julia Morris

What is it for?

This cipher was allegedly used by Julius Caesar to send secret messages to his generals.

It is a simple substitution cipher in which each letter is replaced by another letter.

How do I create it?

Use one of the many templates that can be found online. Cut out the larger and smaller wheel and attached them with a split pin or just place them on top of each other.

To create a digital version, put two copies of the template on a PowerPoint presentation and use "crop to shape" to cut out the smaller disk as a circle. Then place it on the larger one. To create your message, decide on your substitution, e.g. T=A and line up T on the big wheel and A on the small wheel. Spell out your message with the big wheel but write down the letters that the small wheel shows.

How do the students use it?

To decipher a message with the classic Caesar wheel, you need to know (or find out by experimenting), which letter to set it on. In the example above, it is set to "T", meaning T=A, U=B etc., so the word "THE" would be written "A O L". It could use used to decode a short text or definition, and students need to find out what the text is about or what fact in the text is not true. To make it even harder, each word could require the wheel to be turned, but they would need some hint on how to set it for each.

If they are using the paper version, they can physically turn the little wheel, but if they are using the digital version, they need to stay in edit mode in the presentation and click into the centre of the little wheel. They can then see a little white "rotate" arrow that they can use to align the letters. It is important that the two centres of the circles stay on top of each other.

How could I use it?

- Biology: a text describing a process, where one word is wrong – take the first letter of the word to get a code letter or count the letters of the word to get the code number
- Art: The text gives the title of an artwork. Pick out the correct one from a list of painting. Each painting has a different code number attached to it.
- P.E. Three words are decoded that are all associated with a certain sport. Count the letters of the sports to get a code number.

Cryptograms

Resources	paper: worksheet
Question	text
Answer	text

What does it look like?

Image: use puzzlemaker.discoveryeducation.com/

What is it for?

Decipher the text to find the hidden message. Each line has a number or symbol underneath that is associated with a letter.

How do I create it?

The easiest way is to use puzzlemaker.discoveryeducation.com/. It is free and does not require an account. You simply decide if you want to give some letters away, e.g. all vowels like in the second example above, and choose what the letters are replaced with: other letters, numbers, or Greek letters. When the cryptogram has been generated, you can take a screenshot.

The disadvantage of the website is that it does not give the teacher the key to the cryptogram, so you have to work which number stand for which letter yourself, which should not be too difficult if you have the original text. Use the alphabet key template above to fill in letters and keep it safe.

There are different ways of hiding code in the text. The easiest way is to end the text with "code:" followed by a few random letters, which will be the passcode to the next lock (they could also be unjumbled to form a word). When choosing the code letters, make sure they are all included in the text, and some of them ideally only towards the end, so the whole text needs to be solved to find the letters. It is good if the students do not realise where the code will appear in the text. Another way to hide a codeword is to include a mistake in the text that the students have to discover. E.g. Cats are a small species of carnivorous reptiles – the codeword is either reptiles because it is the wrong word or mammals, which is the correct answer. You could also add random letters at the end or in the middle of different words in the text, so students need to collect all of them to get the codeword.

This task is best done on paper; I would only use a short text as a digital task as it is much more difficult to do if you cannot write on the lines. Insert the cryptogram into a presentation but give students some scrap paper to write down the answer.

How do the students use it?

Students will need some clue what the text is about, e.g. you could give them the beginning of a definition, and they have to use the cryptogram to work out the rest. It could also be a translation or a reconstruction of a text they have recently seen.

Cryptograms can also be turned into a group task. Print the cryptogram on one side of a piece of paper and the key to it on the other side and give students an extra sheet to write on. Now one student reads out the numbers of the cryptogram, the other looks up what letter the number corresponds to, and a third student writes down the correct letter.

How could I use it?

- Science: Complete the definition: noble gases are…
- Languages: translate the text
- English: This cryptogram is a summary of the first paragraph of chapter 2.
- Geography: This cryptogram is a postcard of someone describing a certain location. Work out where they are.

Rebus

Resources	digital: Document or presentation paper: worksheet
Question	text, words
Answer	text, word

What does it look like?

w+
b=h
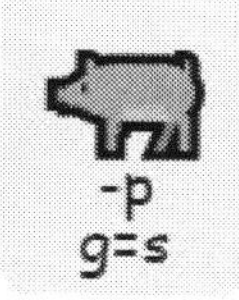
-p
g=s

+is
-ba
Hint 1: You're stuck? Click on an icon to get a different one!
Hint 2: You can download this rebus and do with it whatever you want! Download
Hint 3: Copy the link to this rebus to the clipboard. Click here.

Image: **www.rebus.club**

What is it for?

A rebus is a puzzle that replaces some of the letters with pictures. If the picture does not completely correspond to the word, it will indicate that some letters need to be taken away (as in "pig minus p" is "ig") and other letters need to be added or replaced ("bat b=h" means "hat"). The message in the example spells "What is this".

How do I create it?

You could create the text yourself, using subject-specific images. It is probably easiest to find images first, and then try to think of phrases that can be made from the words that the images represent without having to change too many letters. An easier way is to use an online rebus maker, like www.rebus.club or https://www.festisite.com/rebus/, which will do the work for you and find all the pictures as well. To make it subject-specific, your rebus text could describe a person, object or process linked to your topic, that will provide the codeword or number. It could also give students instructions, e.g. look under the model of a volcano in the classroom,

How do the students use it?

Students replace the pictures with words and follow hints on letter substitution. Then they solve the text-based tasks or follow the instructions the text gives them.

How could I use it?

- Music: Use musical notation to replace letters in words
- Religious Education: Use religious symbols to form words.
- English Language: Work out the rebus and then find a synonym of the word from a list or use the rebus to practise the spelling of difficult words.

Substitution Ciphers

Resources	paper: Worksheet digital: Presentation
Question	text
Answer	text

What does it look like?

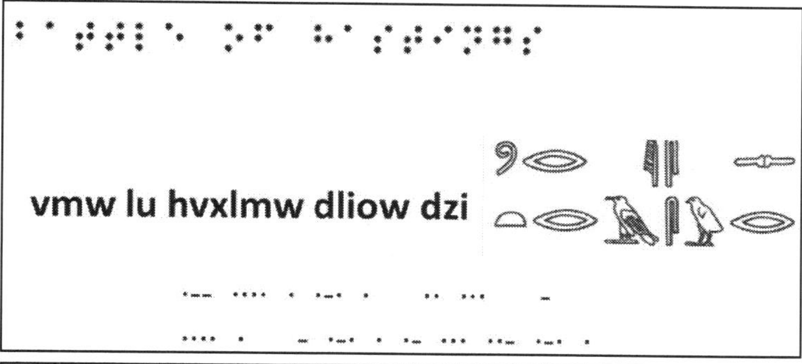

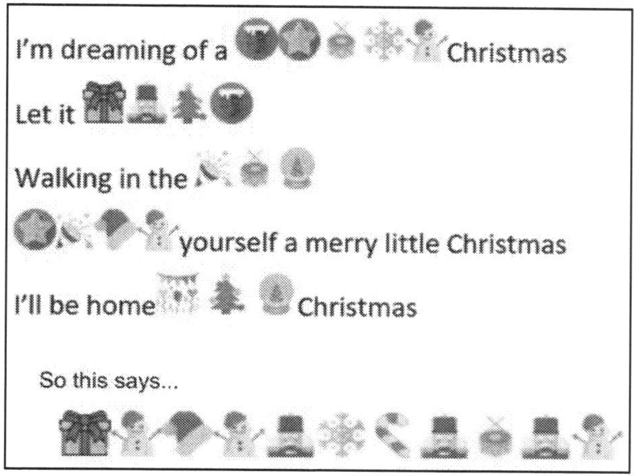

What is it for?

The favourite of all wannabe spies, there are hundreds of substitution ciphers, from hieroglyphs to braille. They are all based on the principle that each letter of the alphabet is replaced with a specific symbol, number or letter.

How do I create it?

There are hundreds of "translators" online, like www.lingojam.com. Many websites allow you to input English text on the one side and then they generate the cipher on the other. Copy and paste or take a screenshot to add it to a worksheet. Most ciphers come with the key, otherwise just put in the whole alphabet to generate a key yourself.

A fun idea for younger students is a Lego cipher, in which each letter is represented by a different combination of Lego bricks. Write out the alphabet on a piece of paper, place different combinations of bricks next to each letter and either take a picture or display in the classroom as the key to a message build from more bricks.

How do the students use it?

As long as the students have the key, it is just a question of spelling out the message by finding each symbol or picture in the list and replacing it with a letter.

How could I use it?

As there are so many different ciphers, it will be relatively easy to find one that fits the theme of your room. Use runes for a history-themed one, or a spy cipher for a WWII or crime one.

Cipher puzzles lend themselves to be combined with other tasks, e.g. finding the alphabet key by searching the room, opening a box or using a QR reader.

How could I use it?

- Students work out the key by answering questions or filling gaps. For example, the second picture above tests students' knowledge of Christmas songs.
- Make multiple-choice questions more interesting by writing them in cipher. The numbers next to the correct answers will form the code.
- Encode a list of words, and the passcode will be what they have in common, e.g. mammals, colours in Spanish
- Encode a whole text that contains a mistake, and the wrong word is the passcode, e.g. "The gunpowder plot was planned by Jacob Fawkes". Answer: Jacob

Acrostics and other fun with words

Resources	digital: Document or presentation paper: worksheet
Question	text
Answer	text

What does it look like?

"An Acrostics" by Edgar Allan Poe

Elizabeth it is in vain you say
"**L**ove not"—thou sayest it in so sweet a way:
In vain those words from thee or L.E.L.
Zantippe's talents had enforced so well:
Ah! if that language from thy heart arise,
Breath it less gently forth—and veil thine eyes.
Endymion, recollect, when Luna tried
To cure his love—was cured of all beside—
His follie—pride—and passion—for he died.

Marley was dead: to begin with. There is no doubt whatever about that. The register of his burial was signed by the clergyman, the clerk, the undertaker, and the chief mourner. Scrooge signed it: and Scrooge's name was good upon 'Change, for anything he chose to put his hand to. Old Marley was as dead as a door-nail.

1/4/1
1/11/8
2/5/3
4/3/2

AXVYEWNZGSEBRPS

CHUOLPCXWO
TSXCOARTYIOJSWJUTXKYOGYERNKWY

What is it for?

There are many ways of hiding messages in a text. The classical one is using acrostics, where the first or last letters in a text, usually a poem, spell out a message.

Another way is to give numbers indicating which line, word and letter to use like in the example above, based on "A Christmas Carol" by Charles Dickens.

The third example shows three words that have extra letters added in between the correct letters. The first word spells "Avengers" if you take every second letter. The second one spells "Coco" if you take every third and the last one spells "Toy Story" with every fourth letter.

How do I create it?

To make an acrostic, decide on the message first and write it from top to bottom, then write a line starting with each of the letters, it does not necessarily have to rhyme and could be based on your subject – you might even be able to adapt a paragraph from the textbook. Make sure that the shape of the text is unusual enough to nudge the students into thinking that there might be something else going on. You could, for example, start each line with a capital letter.

If you use numbers for the hidden words like in the Charles Dickens example, part of the puzzle could be to work out which textbook the message is based on – this could be in the form of another puzzle. To make it a little bit easier, you could add letters:

P: 34 Li:8, W:3 Le:8 (page 34, line 8, word 3, letter 8).

In the third puzzle, the words are easier to find if the topic is given (movie titles in this case) or a hint of how many letters to skip. Again, this could be given as the solution to another puzzle. It also helps if the letters that need to be skipped are less common ones like X, Y, Z. You could even hide two words within each other by interspersing letters.

How do the students use it?

The hardest part for the students in these challenges are to work out what exactly they have to do – once they have worked out the system, finding the letters is just a question of following the pattern and noting them down. Try to avoid giving too many instructions at the beginning – the students will feel great if they discover the "trick" themselves.

How could I use it?

- English: Find the first verb in the text and take the 3rd letter
- History: Find the sentence in the text that shows the political bias of the author and take the last letter of the 4th word.
- Geography: Look at these strange strings of letters. Each hides a word used to describe a factor that influences population growth.

Scytale – wrapped up messages

Resources	paper: strip of paper, tape, cardboard tube or similar, pen
Question	what does the text say?
Answer	words, sentences

What does it look like?

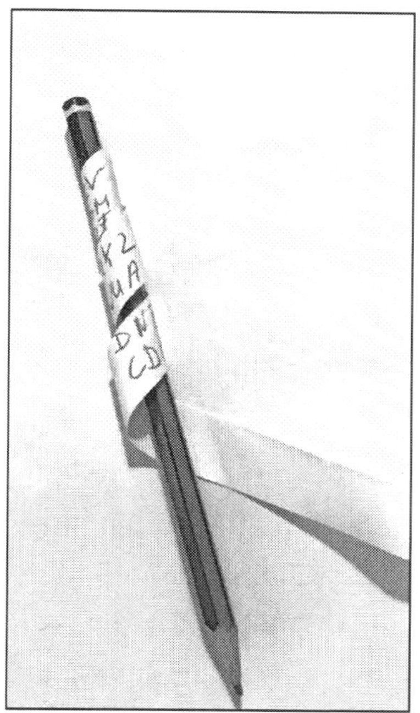

Image: Julia Morris

What is it for?

A scytale is an ancient Greek way of conveying secret messages. The message is written on a long piece of paper (or on a leather belt in Greek times) and can only be read when it is wrapped around a rod of the correct diameter.

How do I create it?

The easiest thing to use as your "rod" is an empty toilet or kitchen paper roll. You can also use a pen, but it makes it more difficult to write the message because it will have to be quite small.

I recommend watching a YouTube video about making a scytale cipher; it will walk you through the steps. Cut off a long thin strip of paper attach it to the very top of the tube with some tape, but so that it is easy to remove again. You could draw a symbol here, half on the paper and half on the tube, to make the starting point obvious. Then wrap the paper all the way down the rod with as little overlay as possible. Secure the end and write a message from the top to the bottom. For longer messages, start the second line back at the top to the right of the first one. Draw several lines from the top to the bottom on the different sides of the tube, to show the students that they have lined it up correctly. Fill the rest of the tube with random letters and numbers.

How do the students use it?

Students get the piece of paper and the tube or they need to find them around the classroom. Part of the challenge is to work out how to use it, but the lines and symbols should help. Once the students have read the words/sentences, then can either use them as a codeword or find matching pictures or definitions in a numbered table to get the passcode.

How could I use it?

- Maths: The message asks the students to calculate the diameter of the tube
- Drama: The message tells them to look under the poster of a certain play where they find the next clue.
- Food: the message consists of the ingredients; students work out which recipe it is

Half text

Resources	paper: worksheet, presentation to create digital: presentation
Question	text
Answer	text

What does it look like?

What is being described here?

is a process used by plants and other organisms to convert light energy into chemical energy that can later be released to fuel the organisms activities (energy transformation). This chemical energy is stored in carbohydrate molecules, such as sugars, which are synthesized from carbon dioxide and water

...form: a genus of spring blooming perennial herbaceous bulbiferous geophytes (having bulbs as storage organs). The flowers are usually large, showy and brightly colored, generally red, pink, yellow, or white (usually in warm colors). They often have a different colored blotch at the base of the tepals (petals and sepals, collectively), internally. Because of a degree of variability within the populations, and a long history of cultivation, classification has been complex and controversial.

What is it for?

This is a simple way of turning any text into a challenge by making either covering half of each line or by mirroring the text and turning it upside-down.

How do I create it?

Insert a text onto a presentation. Change the line spacing to 2.0. Then use "shapes" to insert a long rectangle covering up half of each line, making sure to change the fill and border colour to white. It is astonishing how moving the shapes by a fraction of a centimetre can change the readability of the text, so it is worth playing around with it and making some lines easier and some harder to read.

To create an upside down and backwards text, write your text into a presentation, then run the presentation and take a screenshot of the slide. Insert the screenshot into an empty slide and use the dots on the left or right to pull the image across itself to turn it to mirror writing. To make it even harder, use the arrow or dot at the top to turn the image upside down. For an extra challenge, cover up half of each line as described above. Using both upside-down and backwards writing means that students cannot simply turn the page around or read it by holding it up against the light.

How do the students use it?

Students find the text and read it out loud to each other or copy it out. They then need to figure out what specific term the text defines or do the action that it describes. If you are giving the half-lines text out as a digital task, make sure that you give it out as a screenshot, so students can not just remove the covering up. It is best to give out the upside-down text as a printout so students can not work out how to undo all the turning and reversing.

The hidden text could be combined with another puzzle and give the students the answers for a crossword puzzle, for example.

How could I use it?

- Literature/Art/History: the biography of a famous person
- P.E.: The rules of a ball game
- Business studies/Science: the definition of a technical term

Homophones and words within words

Resources	digital: Document or presentation paper: worksheet
Question	sentence
Answer	words

What does it look like?

I went to the party for an hour and ate all the cake = 248

What is it for?

A classic amongst puzzle enthusiasts is to use homophones – words that sound like other words. Some numbers are easy to hide in a text like in the example above.

one=won

two= to/too

four = for

eight= ate

The rest of the numbers as well as other words might be a bit more difficult. Another way of hiding words is contained in other words like "nine" in "canine" or in a phrase like "one" in "I sO NEarly didn't do it!". There are some nice examples with numbers here: https://www.braingle.com/brainteasers/49386/hidden-numbers.html

How do I create it?

The website https://www.thefreedictionary.com/Word-Finder.htm can be very helpful here. Scroll down to find search boxes for words that "start with", "end with" and "contain". So, if you wanted to hide the word "three" between two words, you could search for a word ending in "th" and another word starting with "ree" and then write a sentence with those two words.

To make it educational, you could try to hide words related to your topic, but that might be quite difficult. Instead, you could hide numbers and then add a numbered table with subject-related pictures or definitions from which the students must choose.

How do the students use it?

Students get the text and maybe a hint to read it out loud or to look for hidden words/numbers. Once they have worked out the words or numbers, they can use them as a passcode or find them in a numbered table that will give them the passcode.

How could I use it?

- English: practice homophones
- Languages: find the hidden numbers in the foreign language
- History: Find the hidden numbers, then find the event in the numbered table. When did the event happen – this is your code number?

Logic Grid Puzzle

Resources	digital: document or presentation paper: worksheet
Question	1-4 categories with several answers each
Answer	choice of short phrases, numbers, pictures

What does it look like?

Four friends are exchanging Christmas presents. Find out who got which present and what their professions are. The presents are a red pen, a brown flowerpot, an orange heart rate monitor and a green toolbox.

No one got anything useful for their job!

Neither George nor Bernard got an orange item.

Ruben sometimes visits the mechanic in his workshop, etc.

	fitness	mechanic	teacher	gardener	brown	green	red	orange
Ruben	O	X	X	X				
George	X							X
Bernard	X							X
Oscar	X							
red								
green								
orange								
brown								

What is it for?

Students need to use hints to work out which items match, and which items exclude each other.

To include an educational aspect, the items and descriptions could be subject related. For example, you could have the names of four people doing different experiments with different chemicals and your clues could be along the line of "Peter uses the chemical that has the highest boiling point but does not conduct an experiment that requires electricity".

How do I create it?

The example above is a simple logic grid puzzle with three categories of words (names, colours, jobs) and four words each. You could have more words or more categories, but it will make creating and solving it a much longer process.

To see more example, have a look at https://www.brainzilla.com/logic/logic-grid/.

Start by choosing your categories and items and decide on a solution and note it down. In the example it would be something like Ruben – gardener - orange; George – mechanic - red etc. Each word can only be used once.

Start by creating a 9x9 table or use the template. Decide on your items, e.g. days of the weeks, locations, sizes. Fill in the words for two of the categories in the left-hand column.

In the top row, you repeat the words of the second category and add the third category.

Now start writing clues. There should be a mix between clues that rule some combinations out and some that establish connections. For example: Neither George nor Bernard got a heart rate monitor – rules out the combination of either of those names with this object. Or more subtly: Ruben sometimes visits the mechanic – this means Ruben is not the mechanic himself. A hint that establishes a connection would be: Ruben loves sport and has made it his profession – means he is the fitness instructor.

Also, try to include hints that are not immediately helpful, e.g. Ruben's present is bigger than Oscar's – this will only be useful after they have worked out what Oscar's present is.

The hints should not be in order of usefulness, so that students must recognise themselves which hints to use first.

How do the students use it?

The players read the clues and if two items exclude each other, put a cross in the box where the two items intersect. If two items match, put a circle. They can then also put crosses in the rest of the row and column because if you know that George is a mechanic, he cannot also be a gardener, and you know that none of the other men is a mechanic as they all have different jobs.

If you know that George is a mechanic, any crosses from the mechanic column will also apply to the George row, e.g. if we know that the mechanic did not get anything red, we also know that George did not get anything red. If a row or column has 3 out of 4 crosses, the last one must be true. This way, students apply all hints until they have found all the connections.

To turn this puzzle into a code, you could combine it with a multiple-choice table:

George is:

a) a mechanic – code 15

b) a gardener – code 13

c) a teacher – code 33

The teacher gets:

a) a flowerpot – code 12

b) a toolbox – code 98

c) a heart rate monitor – code 91

Now add up all codes you have found to get the passcode.

How could I use it?

- History: Which of these (fictional) soldiers fought at which battle and what weapon did they use?
- Art: which person buys which famous building and in which year were they build?
- Maths: which of these graphs represents which survey and what scales have been used?

Word Clouds

Resources	digital: Document or presentation paper: worksheet
Question	text
Answer	words

What does it look like?

Image: www.wordclouds.com

What is it for?

A text is turned into a shape, and the more often the word is used in the text, the larger it is. The first text above is based on the Wikipedia article on lions. The second word cloud is based on a category – in this case "types of blue".

How do I create it?

There are many word cloud generators, like https://www.wordclouds.com/, where you can simply paste a text, and it will generate the "cloud" for you. You can then choose the shape, colours and font. It will automatically take out function words like "the" or "is" because they would otherwise be the largest words but do not really help in working out what is being described. On wordclouds.com, you can also assign a "weight" to every word so that you can make certain words more prominent, even if they do not appear often in the text. This is especially useful for very short texts with no repetition. It also allows you to take out the name of the item you are defining.

How do the students use it?

Students read the words and work out what the category is or what is being described. They can use the word as a password or find it in a numbered table to get a passcode.

How could I use it?

- Religion: a Wikipedia article about a religion
- English: the plot of a book (with the names taken out)
- ICT: The definition of a technical term

Letter Maze

Resources	digital: document or presentation paper: worksheet
Question	follow the text through the maze
Answer	text

What does it look like?

www.festisite.com

What is it for?

Follow the path through the maze to find the hidden sentence. The sentence could describe a process, a formula or a list of words. To get to a code number, you could again combine it with a table of pictures or definitions plus numbers, so once the students have worked out what the maze says, they can find it in the table to get the passcode.

How do I create it?

Use https://www.festisite.com/text-layout/maze/ and enter your sentence or list of words. The longer the text, the bigger and more complex the auto-generated maze. If your text is longer than about 115 characters (including spaces), the maze will automatically have two levels to it, meaning you will have two sheets with two mazes and have to find your way through both to get the full message.

The dead ends of the maze are always filled with the same text, but the sentences will be cut off by the walls.

How do the students use it?

Students start on the left-hand side and try to find their way through the maze to the right. They cannot solve it by following the text alone, as the text is repeated in dead ends. They must solve the maze first, then read the text along the path they have found.

How could I use it?

- Maths: a formula written in words
- English: a list of words – what do they all have in common?
- Science: a list of elements – what is the logical next one?

Cut Out

Resources	digital: presentation paper: worksheet or cardstock, scissors/hole punch
Question	where do you need to line up the "key"?
Answer	numbers/words

What does it look like?

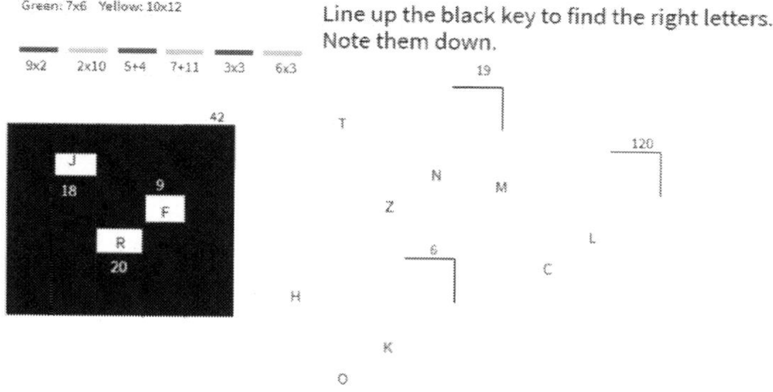

Image: Julia Morris

What is it for?

Students need two pieces of paper (or a moveable digital object) - one with the code, one with holes in it that need to be lined up in the right way to see the code through the holes. The lines at the top give clues where the "key" needs to be lined up to get the right number or letter.

How do I create it?

Decide on the shape of your key – it does not need to be square and could even be someone's face with holes instead of eyes or mouth.

If you are creating a paper version, draw or print your key onto sturdy paper and cut out the holes or punch them out with a hole punch. Now lay your key onto different places on the background paper and trace a little bit of the outline, just enough to help line up the key in the right position, and write your code numbers or letters into the holes as well as some extra ones as red herrings.

Draw lines in different colours at the top and think of a category for each colour and label the places where the key must be lined up with words from the same category. Optionally, you can label the holes in the key as well and then give a hint for each line, so students must decide which hole to look through.

If you are creating a digital activity, create the key by placing several of rectangles of different length next to each other (see below), then left-click and draw a box around them to group them. Now you can change the fill and outline colour to the same colour to make it look like one piece with holes in it.

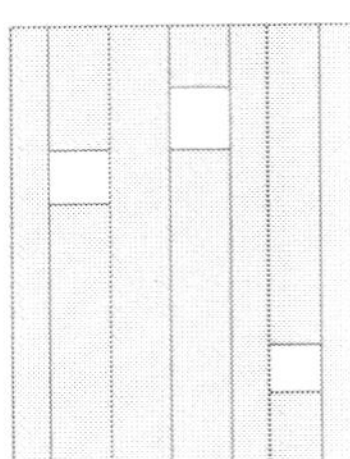

The S'cape website also has a handy tool to create a strip of black and white blocks that are revealed to be letters if seen through a cut-out. See here for examples: https://scape.enepe.fr/scrypto.html

You can create the activity with their online tool: https://scape.enepe.fr/ressources/scrypto/, simply change the text in the first text box and click the printer. To print the black overlay, enable background printing in the printer settings.

How do the students use it?

In the example, the "key" is the black square. The coloured lines give clues on where to find the letters. "Green:7x6" means that the square must be lined up with the corner that says 42 next to it. The first green line says "9x2", so they need the letter that you can see through the hole with 18 next to it. The next line is yellow, so the black key needs to be moved around to line up with the corner that says 120 next to it and so on. Students note down the letters or numbers that they see through the hole to get a passcode, or they click on the letters in a digital version.

If you are using a digital PowerPoint or Google presentation, students will have to stay in edit mode to be able to move the key around, and in a Genial.ly presentation, you need to turn "drag elements" in settings on.

How could I use it?

- Physical Education: Line up the key with different parts of a skeleton
- Geography: Line up the key with different parts of a water cycle
- English: Line up the key in the shape of Shakespeare's head with the word in the scene that means...

Scratch Card and Hidden Pictures

Resources	digital: presentation or Genial.ly account paper: printed paper, acrylic paint, washing up liquid, brush, clear tape.
Question	what is hidden here
Answer	words, numbers, pictures

What does it look like?

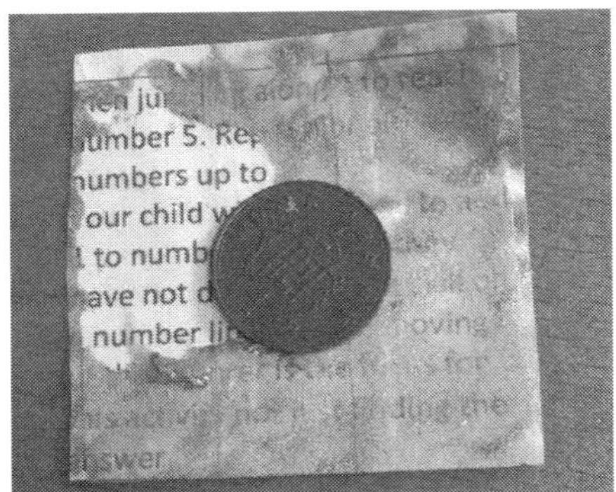

Image: Julia Morris

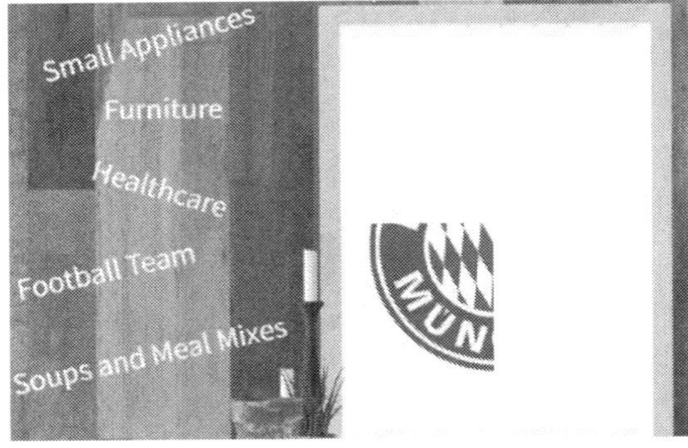

Image: Genial.ly

What is it for?

Everyone loves the thrill of a scratch card, discovering what is hidden behind that silver square if it is a winner. You can make paper scratch cards yourself without too much effort, but they can only be used once. You can also make digital activities that are similar in that the picture or word has to be discovered behind some plain coloured boxes.

Anything could be in a scratch card: a text, picture, instructions to the next step or even a QR code. In a digital activity like in the one above, you could have a list of options next to the hidden picture and students can click on the correct answer.

How do I create it?

There are lots of YouTube videos on making scratch cards, for example, https://youtu.be/P0xDwDYC4Hw. All you need is a piece of paper with the secret message written or printed on it. Cover it in clear tape. Then you mix a spoon full of acrylic paint (silver is most realistic) with a little bit of washing up liquid (advice online ranges from a few drops to 1:1) and paint over the tape, you might need several layers to cover it, but you can do lots of tickets at the same time.

To create a digital scratch card on, you can use www.Genial.ly, PowerPoint or Google slides, although the latter has the least options.

For all three versions, insert the object or text you want to hide into your slide. Then create a square, by inserting a shape. The square should be much smaller than the original picture, a quarter of the size of the full picture or less.

If you are using Genial.ly, select the shape and the animation symbol above it, select "hover mouse" and "hide". Now the square will disappear if you slide your mouse or finger over it and reveal a part of the picture behind it. Copy and paste the square as many times as needed to cover up the picture but keep in mind that only one square at a time will be invisible, so only small parts of the picture can be seen.

If you are using PowerPoint, select the square, and in the animation tab, choose one of the exit animations like "disappear". Now choose "Trigger" in the animation tab and choose "on the click of" and the name of the square, normally "rectangle 1". Now copy and paste the squares to cover up the picture. In presentation mode, you can now click any square and it will disappear, so more and more of the picture will be revealed.

In Google slides, create a square, right-click it and choose "animate". In the taskbar on the right choose "add animation" and choose an exit effect like "fly out" and "on click". Unfortunately, animations do not get copied with the object, so you will have to add the animation to each object individually. When the presentation is run, the boxes disappear in the order in which you have added the exit effects, so it might be good to add them in a random order so that maybe the top middle square disappears first, then the bottom right-hand corner one etc. to make it more challenging to guess the picture.

How do the students use it?

If using real scratch cards, the students will need something like a coin to scratch away the top layer and reveal the question or hint. In the digital version, they uncover the image until they have enough information to click the correct answer from a list of options to get to the next task.

How could I use it?

- Design Technology: pictures of different tools or artists
- Physics: a picture of an experiment set up
- English: A famous quote – who said it?

Text Wheel

Resources	paper: printout, scissors, split pin
Question	words, text
Answer	words, numbers, pictures

What does it look like?

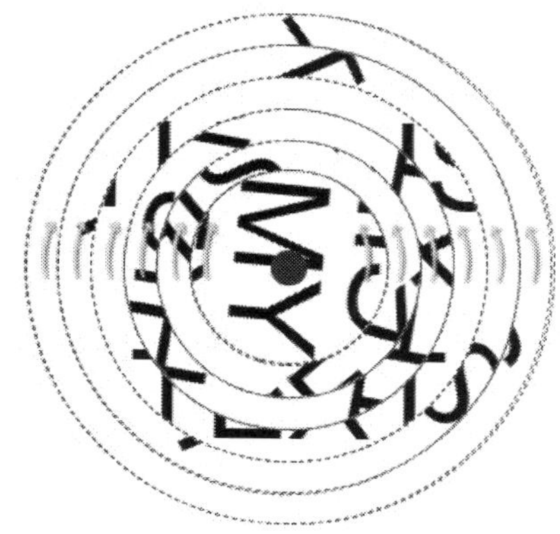

Image: scape.enepe.fr/

What is it for?

Disguise a text or picture by spreading it over multiple stacked wheels.

How do I create it?

The easiest way to create a wheel with text is to design and print a template on http://scape.enepe.fr/ressources/concentrx/ccx-txt.html. Write your text into the first text box and use the second one to choose lower- or upper-case letters. The other options are the text size, line spacing space, offset, font and number of wheels. Tick the box at the bottom if you want each wheel to be printed on a new page to avoid cut off circles. Once you have printed and cut the circles, attach them with a split pin or hide the wheels separately around the room for the students to assemble themselves.

If you want to integrate the wheel into a digital presentation, the S'cape website also offers a tool for creating a Genial.ly picture wheel. You can find presentation with instructions in the link collection.

If you want to use the wheel with a picture or screenshot of an online text, use the template or create a presentation with the picture in the back, a larger ring (a circle without fill) and a smaller circle that is fill in white in the middle. This way, you can only see the outer part of the picture. Repeat on the next slide with a smaller ring and circle but keep the picture in the same size and the centre of the circle in the same place in relation to the picture. Repeat until you have enough wheels, print, cut and attach.

How do the students use it?

Students turn the wheels until they can read the text or recognise the picture and are able to answer the questions about it.

How could I use it?

- Science: Which process is described in the text?
- Art: find five things that should not be on this painting.
- English: In which of the books in the bookshelf would you find this text? The next clue is waiting on the page that the text came from.

DIGITAL PUZZLES

Learningapps, Bookwidgets and S'cape

Resources	digital only, can be embedded in Google sites, Genial.ly or linked from other documents and presentations
Question	various
Answer	various

What does it look like?

LearningApps:

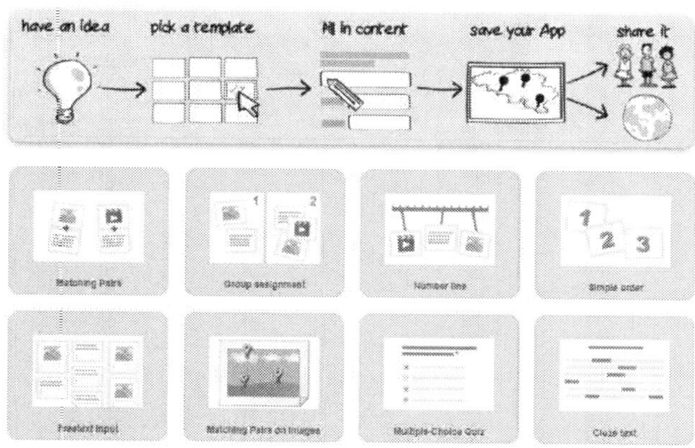

Bookwidgets:

What is it for?

Learningapps and Bookwidgets are two websites that offer the teacher the opportunity to create a range of different online activities like gap fill, match up and crossword puzzles. Both allow the teacher to write their own feedback or "reward word" which the students receive only after they have completed an activity, and which can contain a password or clue.

LearningApps is a free website run by an educational charity, while Bookwidgets is a paid-for subscription. Both websites generate a unique link to the activity which can be integrated into your escape room and LearningApps also gives you an embed code so that the activities can appear directly in a Google site or a Genial.ly presentation.

S'cape is a website run by a group of teachers from France who have created a lot of interesting resources for digital escape rooms (https://scape.enepe.fr/-les-outils-s-cape-.html). Unfortunately, the website is only available in French at the moment. Still, by using the translator build into your web browser (normally an icon within the address bar), you can find your way around, even if you do not speak any French – and it is worth it! On the site, you can find templates to print out – some of which are included in this puzzle chapter - and there are digital tools that can be used in Google sites or Genial.ly. The most versatile of those are dice https://scape.enepe.fr/dede.html and a timer https://scape.enepe.fr/ressources/minuteur/. The website offers many very useful add-ons for Genial.ly like tick boxes, password check and drag and drop. Templates and videos explaining how to use them can be found in this presentation by Marie Allirot and me: https://view.genial.ly/5f3ba271df60d90d8a0efda6/interactive-content-scape-tools-for-genially

The developers of S'cape have made their tools available for free for teachers but ask that they are not used for commercial use.

How do I create it?

To use LearningApps or Bookwidgets, the teacher will need to create a free account, but students will not need one to access the activity.

Choose one of the many activities like "match up", "find in the picture" or "sort by category". The pictures above only show a part of the activities available. Fill in your content in the form of words, numbers and pictures and even YouTube video clips and auto-generated text to speech. The most important part is to fill in the feedback box with the codeword (and tell students to write it down – otherwise they must do the whole activity again). Then have a look at the preview and save the app. It will then give you a link or an embed code to the activity. Use the full-screen link for the best experience if you are not embedding.

How do the students use it?

Students follow the link and read the instructions that you have written for them when creating the app. In the end, they click the checkmark icon in the bottom right to get the feedback box with the next hint or passcode.

How could I use it?

- History: Watch the YouTube video and fill in the gap text
- Geography: Match the name of the geographical feature to the correct part of the picture
- Languages: Listen to the French numbers and pin them to the correct place on the number line.

360 Degree Views

Resources	digital: website (can be embedded)
Question	questions about the scene
Answer	numbers, words

What does it look like?

Image: https://poly.google.com/creator/tours

What is it for?

Immerse students in a place with 360-degree pictures. Student can look in all directions to feel they are in the scene. The most obvious use is in geography, history, art and language lessons, but there are lots of museums, attractions and sights available, from Harry Potter World to the Great Barrier Reef. A list of amazing places photographed by Google can be found here: https://artsandculture.Google.com/project/street-view All these places can also be found from within Google Maps and Google tour creator.

There are four pages that I have used for this, Google street view, Google VR Tour Creator, 360cities.net and YouTube. All four can also be viewed through VR Googles if you have got them available.

Most teachers and students will be familiar with Google street view. When using Google maps, you can pick up a little yellow man and drop him on the map to look at the location in 360 degrees. This can be useful if you want students to "walk" along a road and explore the area independently because they can use the white arrows on the ground to move forwards and backwards. The disadvantage is that they could get "lost" or miss important sights by speeding down the road. If you want to share specific locations with students and you have a Google account, you can create "my maps". Go to https://www.google.co.uk/maps/ and open the side bar by clicking the three lines next to the search box. Click on "Your places" and the "Maps" tab. At the bottom you can now click "create map" and it will open a new window. Now change the title from "untitled map" to your own title and search for your first place. Once you have found it, the pop-up box will give you the option to "add to my maps". Once you have added all places, click "share" underneath the title and the setting to "everyone with the link". When students open the link, they can see a list of the places and can then click "open in Google maps" to be able to look at them in full detail and with Google street view (if the location allows it). You can do a similar project on Google Earth https://www.google.co.uk/intl/en_uk/earth/, which has impressive satellite pictures and ready-made location information, but to view the places from a mobile device, students would need to download the free Google Earth app.

For a more controlled experience that works on any mobile device, use Google VR tour creator (https://arvr.Google.com/tourcreator/). It allows you to choose any Google street view location and add them to your tour. The students can only see places that have been added, and you can add points of interest: an information box added to a point in the scene with information or a question. You can also add pictures, like in the example above where a picture of the Berlin Wall is layered over the present-day scene to show where it used to stand.

360cities.net is a collection of pictures by independent photographers. They are mostly high-quality photos and are a good option if you are looking for a more specific indoor place or a picture from an event, e.g. carnival in Venice or inside CERN. The link to specific scenes can be shared with the students. You will need to explain to students that white arrows on the ground will take them to a different view of the same place, but blue arrows will take them to a completely different place and should not be clicked.

Not everyone might be aware that YouTube offers a wide range of 360-degree films as well, including city sightseeing and videos of dinosaurs or Vikings. Type in your place or topic followed by "360" and you might get something interesting. While watching the video, you can move the screen and look in all directions. These videos offer high levels of immersion but are not adaptable.

How do I create it?

Use the websites above to find the right locations. Most of them can be embedded in websites or you can share a link. You can then create questions that force students to look around the scene and notice certain things. If you want it to create a passcode, you could limit it to number questions, e.g. how many bicycles can you see under the Eiffel tower. To use other types of questions, you could combine it with another puzzle, e.g. a crossword puzzle or a gap-fill text on learningapps.org to generate a code.

If you are using Google VR Tour Builder, the questions or codes can be put straight into the picture as a point of interest.

How do the students use it?

Students follow the link to the video, picture and tour and look around to answer questions about the scene.

How could I use it?

- biology https://www.360cities.net/image/natural-history-museum-dublin
- physicshttps://www.360cities.net/image/uq-physics-museum or https://www.360cities.net/image/cern-open-days-lhcb
- history: https://www.360cities.net/image/brewhouse-remains-white-castle-wales
- art: https://www.360cities.net/image/american-new-york-the-metropolitan-museum-of-art-1the-european-sculpture-art-central-park
- English: https://www.360cities.net/image/shakespeares-globe-theater1-london

Digital Variations on Multiple-choice

Resources	digital: presentations (some only work in Genial.ly)
Question	multiple-choice
Answer	choice of short phrases, numbers, pictures

Overview

Multiple-choice questions are the easiest type of task to create in online presentation as you can simply add a link to the next page to the right answer, but they are not very fun in themselves and in my opinion should not be used as the main basis of an escape room. There are, however, some ways of making them more entertaining by adding a twist. These ideas work best in Genial.ly, but some include options for other presentations.

The Race (Genial.ly, PowerPoint, Google Slides)

Image: Genial.ly

What is it for?

A simple, stop motion race where the cars, boats, runners etc. move closer to the finishing line with every correct answer.

How do I create it?

Genial.ly offers several nice templates for this, some of which are free. If you want to create your own, simply choose some clipart pictures of your racers and place them on the left-hand side of the slide with the multiple-choice question and options at the bottom. Add a link to the next slide the correct answer by right-clicking on it and choosing “link” or using the link icon in Genial.ly. Wrong options can be linked back to the starting slide to avoid random guessing. On the next slide, move all racers slightly to the right, some a bit further than others. To create excitement, you could make it look as if our racer was about to lose until the last minute. Add a “fly in from left” animation to all racers to give the game a more dynamic feel.

Falling Answers (Genial.ly, PowerPoint, Google Slides)

Image: Genial.ly

What is it for?

Students have time to read the question, but once they click “start”, the multiple-choice answers fall one from the top to the bottom of the screen and disappear. The students need to read them quickly and remember them to be able to click the correct one of the letters that appear after the answers are gone.

How do I create it?

Create one slide with the question and a start button, that links to the next slide. On the next slide, add the multiple-choice answers, but outside the slide at the bottom, the correct answer needs to link to the next slide. Add a “fly in from top” animation to the answers. In

Google Slides choose "after previous", in PowerPoint "with previous" and add a 0.5-second delay. Add the same time delay in Genial.ly. Add just the options (A, B, C, D) and animate them to appear after the flying answers have fallen out of the slide. You should also add a "missed it?" button to your slide that appears at the same time as the option and that links back to the first slide with the question, so students can watch the animation several times if necessary.

The Memory game (Genial.ly, PowerPoint, Google Slides)

Image: Genial.ly

What is it for?

The game starts on a slide that allows students to look at all available answers, without knowing what the question will be. When they click "I'm ready", it takes them to a slide that only shows them the question and the blank back of the answer cards. Now the students not only have to know the answer but also remember where it is hidden. When they click the correct card, they are taken to the next slide.

How do I create it?

On the first slide, add square shapes as the cards and fill them with your words or pictures. If you are working in Genial.ly, you could give it an extra twist by adding another square on top of it and add a "hover over" animation that hides the "back" of the card when you move your mouse over it, so you can only look at one card at a time.

Add a "Ready" button that links to the next slide. On the second slide, add a question and replace all answer cards with cards that only show a plain back. Now add an invisible link to the card that hides the right answer. It could take the player straight to the next question or a slide that reveals all the answers again, to make the next question easier. It is also good to add some feedback, for example, "Correct!" flying past or a green checkmark appearing on the card.

Speed answers (Genial.ly, PowerPoint)

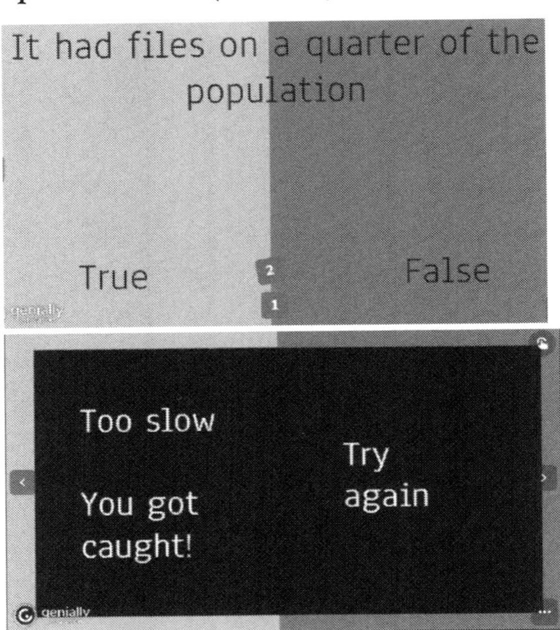

What is it for?

Show a timer at the same time as the multiple-choice question, when the timer is up, the question disappears, and the students must start again.

How do I create it?

It works best with quick true/false questions, and the area that needs to be clicked should be as large as possible as it can be very frustrating for students if they lose just because they clicked outside the right area in their rush.

To create a 3-second timer, add numbers 1,2,3 to the slide and animate them with a time delay so that the number 3 vanishes straight away, number 2 vanishes after one second and 1 vanishes after two seconds. Add a large area that covers all options and that appears after four seconds. It needs to link back to the first slide. If there is more reading to do or more options, you could, of course, create a longer timer.

Flashing answers (Genial.ly, PowerPoint)

What is it for?

The multiple-choice answers are not all visible at the same time but flash on and off and need to be clicked quickly before they disappear. It will work best if the answers are very similar, so students need to remember all the options to decide on the best one.

How do I create it?

In PowerPoint, add the question and then create rectangular shapes all over the page to put the answers in, so you can add invisible links. If you add a link straight to a text, it will always be visible by being underlined and blue and the effect looks the best if the boxes are the same colour as the background so it looks as if the words are appearing out of nowhere. Add a slow animation to all answers, I have used "wipe" and set the duration to 4.50. For all answers, right-click on the animations in the animation pane, select "timing" and change "repeat" to "until end of slide". Also change all to "start with previous" but add a delay of varying lengths for all answers apart from the one you want to appear first, this way they will flash up one after another.

In Genial.ly, the effect looks better if you cover the answers with squares that flash on and off so that the answers are hidden for longer than if you apply the animation to the words itself. Put your answers all over the slide and create rectangles that have the same colour as the background and cover up all the words. Add a "continuous" "fade-in-out" animation to all boxes. Also, add an "entrance" "fade in" animations to all boxes and answers and set varying start times, with about 0.3-sec difference between each other. Answers should have the same start time as the box that is covering them, otherwise all answers will be visible at the beginning.

Sliding background (Genial.ly)

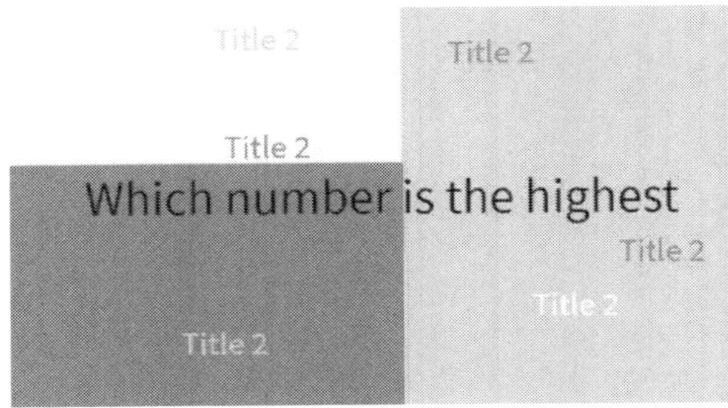

What is it for?

In Genial.ly, you can take advantage of some of the animated backgrounds to get a similar "flashing answers" effect, in which the answers are visible at different times.

How do I create it?

Go into "backgrounds" "library" and select the "animated" tab at the top. Select a background, for example, the one above, and add answers in the same colours as the sliding background tiles, so they are invisible when the background changes. If you are struggling to create exactly the same colour as the background, take a screenshot and save it and upload it to imagecolorpicker.com. It will then show you an HTML/HEX code, starting with #, which you can copy and paste into the first box in the colour creator in Genial.ly.

EXAMPLE ESCAPE ROOMS

In this chapter, I will walk you through two escape rooms to give you some ideas about how they are structured and show some puzzle examples. The first example is a mixed media library induction; the second one is a digital activity for learning the numbers in German. Both are aimed at 12-15-year olds.

Example 1: Library induction

Overview

The game took about 20-30 min and was designed to help 13-year old students who are new to the school to find their way around the library and use the book classifications. The students played the activity in groups of three with one laptop per group. The puzzles were presented on Google site with Google forms acting as the logs. The design of the website was minimal as the focus was to get the students to move around the room and explore the services that the library has on offer.

Planning

In the first stage, I met up with the librarian and discussed what we wanted students to learn from the activity: how to use the Dewy decimal system to find books on a shelf, the thematic layout of the library, how to use the online catalogue, what items are for sale, how to interpret the colours and symbols on the signs and where to find important places like the returns box and the lockers.

The library has a set of laptops for research so we decided to use them as the locks as it would allow all teams to check their answers at the same time and we would not need to spend any money on hardware. I then tried to find a story that would involve the library and the use of computers and at the same time be motivating for the students. I reckoned that the story "The library is in danger of closing

– save the book" would leave many of the students cold, while a story that involved destroying the school network and stopping them from using their phones in school would really get them going!

We drew up a list of learning objectives and matched them to possible puzzles, but in the end, we did not use all of them due to time or technical restraints. Here is the first draft of the overview.

name	**medium**	**task**	**answer**	**Learning objective**
how many	paper/room	find items from picture and count	number code	where to find useful objects
micro-pictures	paper/room	work out what close-ups of items are, find them, and there are numbers/letters on them (paper cutter, return box)	number code	library items
cryptogram	paper/books	find a number of a book, put their Dewey code into cryptogram alphabet to get a word	word	Dewey
snote	paper/posters	look at snote to find different Dewey codes	numbers	categories of posters

		for this category, put them in code breaker, snote words: history, technology, sports etc		
word strips	computer	gives them a book title that they have to find in the catalogue	in the catalogue, it will link to new puzzle	online catalogue
returns	room	put a brown piece of paper in the returns box to create a secret compartment for a key	key	returns box
Bar code scanner	room/compute r	scan book to find more information	publishin g date?	use scanner on book barcodes
final task	room	old phone in locker with prize	need a number code to open locker	

Once we had a definite list of six puzzles that we wanted to use, I walked around the library to choose books and other items to be part of the puzzles, and I tried to spread the locations over as much as the room as possible. I then created a form for each challenge and embedded each form in one page of a simple Google site, all linked to the story by a short message from our "villain":

H@cker Hunt
Call me Mad H@cker... I can write any code, I can break any code... can U?

CODE

*Required

Find book 910.483: there are two red 7-20-12-6-7 on the spine of the book *

Your answer

Find book 895.7: There is a 13-12-20-0-6-21-1-16-16-12-6 on the cover *

Your answer

At 811DIC there are several books on E.Dickinson. Miss Dickinson's FIRST name has 11-24-19-2 letters. *

Your answer

7-18-24 11-24 ? *

Your answer

The second section of each form contained the link to the next page, which was only accessible if all answers in the first sections were correct.

We then realised that it might end up in chaos, if each of the five teams tried to grab the same book at the same time and that teams could simply follow other teams and copy what they do, so I created five copies of the website and the forms so that different groups could solve the tasks in a different order. It made the creation more complex, and the last puzzle in each version had to be adapted, so they all ended with the same code to the same locker to be able to win the prize. It did help to use PowerPoint SmartArt to create a colour-coded overview for each team:

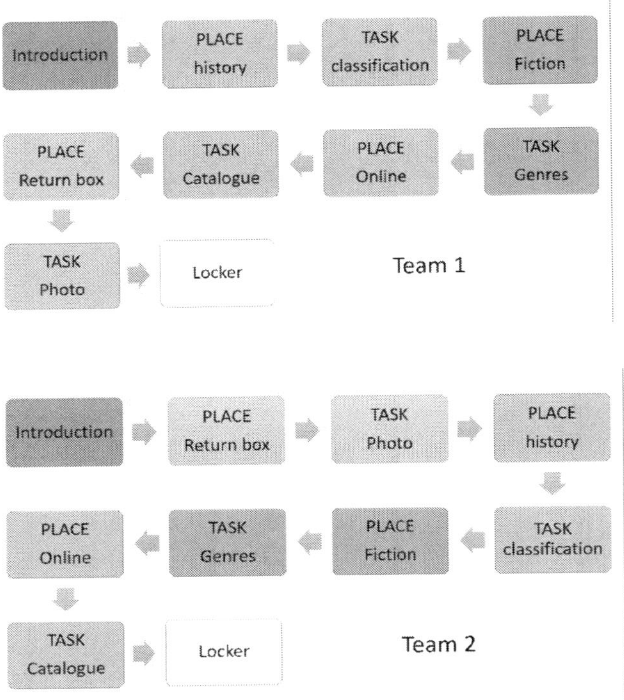

Conducting the game

In the beginning, the students listened to a presentation about the library, the catalogue and the various things they can do in the library.

Then they watched the introductory video (https://youtu.be/oFSuEP-F4eE) which explains that a hacker wants to release a computer virus in 30 minutes to shut down the school network and they have to stop him. Each team was then allocated some notepaper and a laptop that had one of the five versions of the website running, so they all started with a different task.

The classification

```
Call me Mad H@cker... I can write any code,
I can break any code... can U?
```

- `Find book 910.453: there are two red 7-20-12-6-7 on the spine of the book`

- `Find book 595.7: There is a 13-12-20-2-6-21-1-16-16-12-6 on the cover`
- `At 811DIC there are several books on E. Dickinson. Miss Dickinson's FIRST name has 11-24-19-2 letters.`
- `7-13-24   11-24?`

One of the main aims of the activity was for students to learn how the numbering of the books works and where the different topics can be found. In this task, they had to find books with certain classifications and find out what is on the title picture or spine. They did not need to take the book off the shelf as other teams had to find it, too. This was the main point that went wrong when playing the game, though, as students still took books and left them lying around on tables or put them back in the wrong place.

Once they had found the words for the first three questions, they could use the number code to find the last codeword. For example, the first answer is "stars", so 7 = s, 20 = t, 12 = a etc.

The codeword is Sci-Fi, which leads nicely to the next topic, the symbols in the fiction area.

Genres

`So U think number codes are easy? What about this?`

`First letter of the first. Second letter of each of the middle ones. Last letter of the last.`
`What is the codeword?`

In the second task, the students got the pictures used for literary genres in the fiction area. They had to run to the poster which shows that the first picture is "Crime" (letter C), the second is Romance (letter O) etc. which gives them the codeword "colour", which was the next learning objective.

The Colours

```
So U want MORE colours...? Are U sure...?
Philosophy
Cinema/TV
Industry
Animals
What is the colour code?
Y=yellow, P=pink, B=blue, G=green
```

Students had to find the colours of the category signs that are placed above the shelves by walking around to find the different subjects and get the solution GYPB (Green, Yellow, Pink, Blue)

The Catalogue

```
Ok, I get it, U are good at cracking codes.
But can U hack the net like the Mad H@cker?
I love messing with the library catalogue...
You probably don't even know where to find it!
```

- Autobiography - 8th book - title - 2nd word - 1st letter
- Nazis - 3rd book - title - 2nd word - first letter
- Europe- 2nd book - "class" number - last digit
- Waves - first book- author's first name - 1st letter
- Dada - 6th book- "class" number - middle digit
- What word does that spell?

The task included a link to the online library catalogue, and students had to enter the keyword in the search box online to find the correct letters and numbers. They find "p h 0 t 0" which leads to the word photo and the hacker's message "So u want a photo of me?!" and the link to the next task.

The Photo

```
Code?
You might need to go to have a look...
```

Image: Julia Morris

The page simply showed a photo of the book return box and the students could see that there is a small round opening with a lid on the side. When they opened it on the real box, they found a number code inside.

Shopping

```
U won't leave me alone, will U?
First let's go on a shopping trip together!
First digits only!
metal compass- glue stick - eraser - poly pockets
What is the code?
```

Our library sells some stationery. The students had to find the price list and take the first digit of the price of each item in the list to get the code.

The End

```
Did you really get me?!
3948
```

Image: Julia Morris

After solving all six challenges, the students found a photo of a mobile phone locker in the library and the code to open it. Inside the locker, they found a memory stick with the "virus" and a small prize.

Conclusion

Looking back at how the activity went, it was a good decision to make students run through the tasks in a different order, even though it made it more difficult for the staff to see which teams were falling behind. In a couple of sessions, the groups ran out of time, and with this setup, it was hard to determine the winning team quickly. Still, it meant that teams were more evenly spread around the room and did not get in each other's way.

In most sessions, the accompanying English teachers put the students into mixed ability groups which lead to more overall engagement and a closer race to the finish. In the session where students were allowed to choose their teammates, the activity did not always work as smoothly as we ended up with some very strong teams who raced ahead while other teams were very weak and struggled with the puzzles or did not engage with the activity.

Overall, the task was successfully played by over 440 students, and most were more engaged and motivated compared to the year before when classes had to do a more traditional picture treasure hunt around the library, without a story or puzzles.

Example 2: German numbers digital game

In this chapter, I will go through another example, this time a virtual escape room made with Genial.ly for practising the numbers in German. I created a purely digital version during lockdown, but I have now adapted it and added some paper elements for students to play in class. The escape room can be found here: https://view.genial.ly/5ef8e035394ab40d87b472e9/game-breakout-alien-uber-deutschland

All images: Genial.ly

The Communication Centre

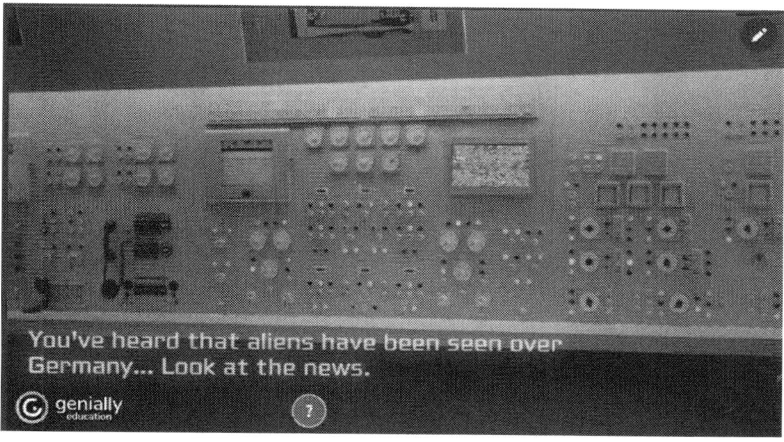

The game starts in the communications room, with a flickering monitor that plays the introduction video on YouTube: https://youtu.be/la5OiTkbBuM. The story is that a UFO has been spotted over Germany and you have managed to sneak into a secret government facility to find out if the aliens have been hidden there.

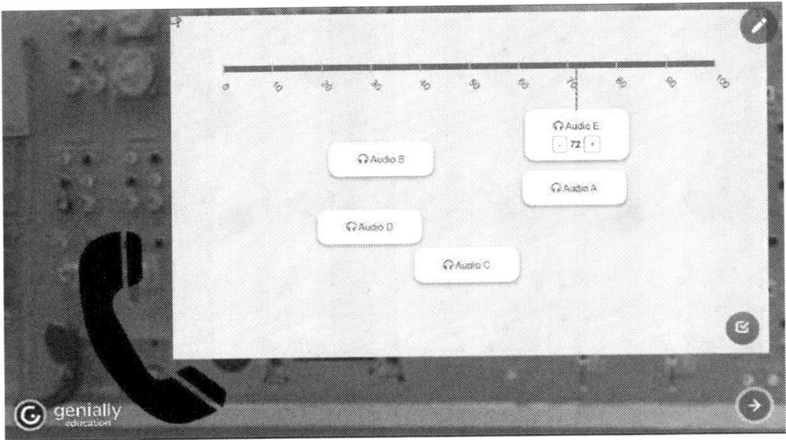

Players look around the communication centre and find a ringing phone, that starts a listening task in which they need to match up spoken numbers in German to a timeline. When the task is completed, the feedback box gives them the first code number. The task was created by embedding a LearningApps activity (instructions in the chapter on LearningApps and Bookwidgets).

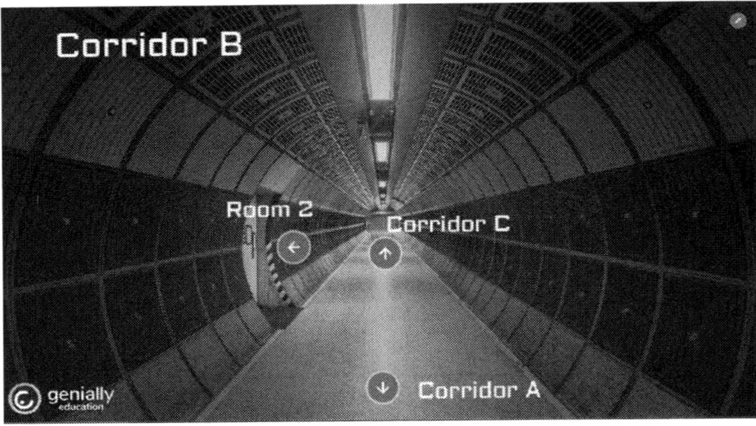

Players can now walk down several corridors to take them to different rooms around the facility. The two pictures above are examples, but I have not included all pictures here.

There were three considerations for me choosing the different rooms, like the accounting office, the map room and the control room: 1. what rooms would you find in a science facility, 2. what rooms match the puzzles and 3. what pictures are available from pixabay within Genial.ly.

Technically, the puzzles can be solved in any order, as students can keep following the corridor. They are more likely to visit each room as they walk past it, but if they get stuck with an activity, they could come back to it later.

Whenever players make a mistake, they "trigger the alarm" and will have to wait 10 seconds for the "try again" button to appear. It will always take them to the first task in the current activity, so if there are five questions in a challenge, they will have to start from the first one, even if they make a mistake on the last one. This makes creating the game easier for the teacher as only one "alarm" slide is needed for each task. It also discourages guessing as it should be quicker to work out the answer than to wait and restart with each mistake.

The Conference Room

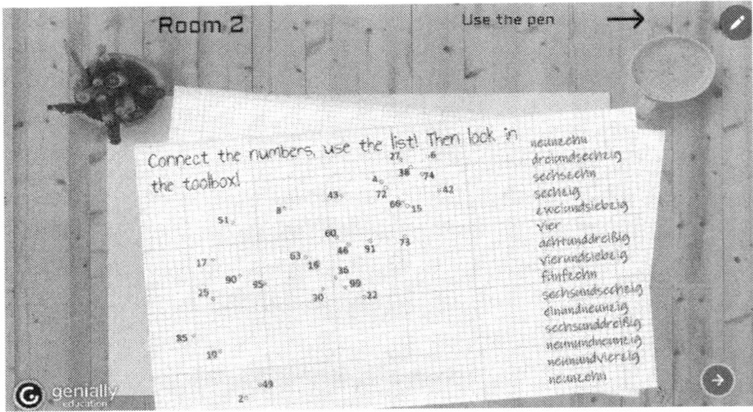

In the conference room, students find a dot to dot activity in German. They will need to translate the numbers on the list, which are in a random order, and then draw the lines, starting at 19, then 63, 16... This activity would work better as a printed version, but during remote learning, the students were able to complete it by using the drawing tool built into Genial.ly.

When all the numbers have been connected (not all of the dots are used), they show the picture of a screwdriver.

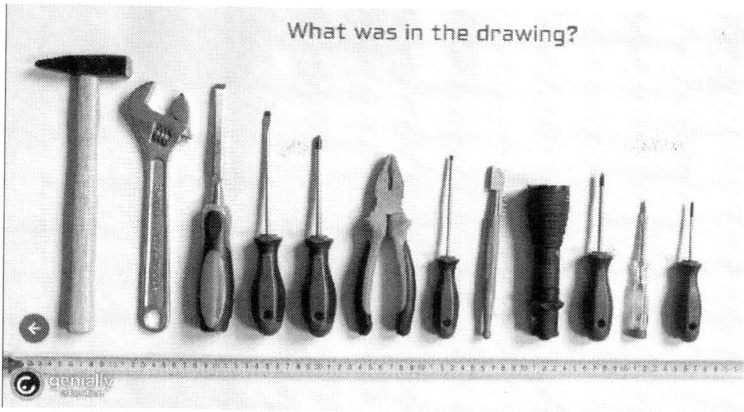

In the conference room is also a toolbox and students can click on the screwdriver to find the measurement underneath which gives them the second code number.

The Accounting Office

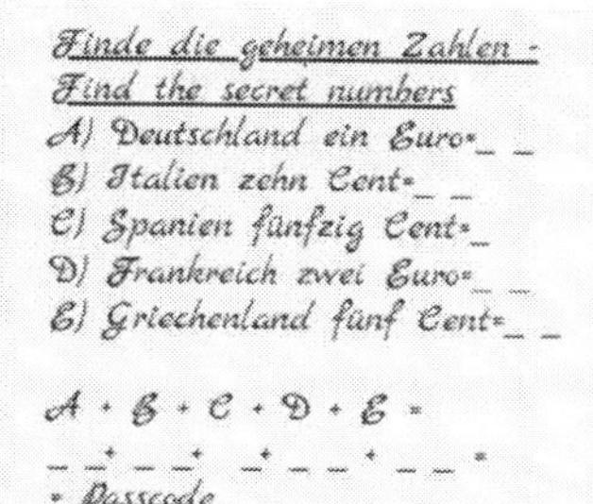

Finde die geheimen Zahlen -
Find the secret numbers
A) Deutschland ein Euro= _ _
B) Italien zehn Cent= _ _
C) Spanien fünfzig Cent= _
D) Frankreich zwei Euro= _ _
E) Griechenland fünf Cent= _ _

A + B + C + D + E =
_ _ + _ _ + _ + _ _ + _ _ =
= Passcode

In the accounting office, there are many euro coins on the table, and when you hover over them, the backside of the coin is revealed as well as a code number. Players need to find the post-it note that tells them which coins to find. The aim of this activity is to make students familiar with the different Euro denominations and teach them that each EU country has different pictures on their coins even though they are all using Euros. The blue book in the corner links to a website with an overview of all coins.

The Office

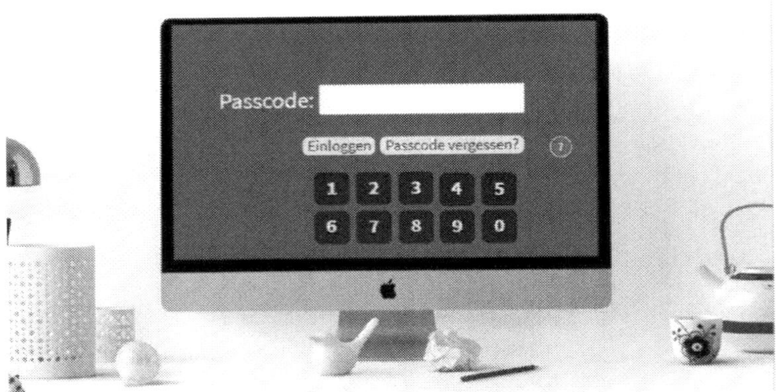

In the office, students need to log into the computer, but they do not know the passcode, so they need to look at the passcode reminder below.

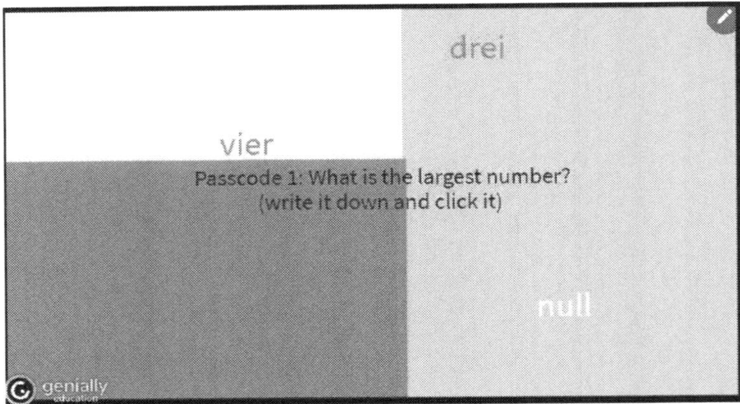

The background in the four slides of this puzzle is animated with coloured blocks moving across the screen so that some of the words cannot be read as they have the same colour. Students have to wait to see all the numbers on the screen and then remember which one the largest one is.

The Archive

In the archive, there is a box of mixed "authentic" documents: a wanted poster, a plane ticket, a concert ticket and a newspaper article that all hint at alien sightings. Each document has a date, and there is a note that indicates that the dates form a pattern.

By reading all documents, students realise that the aliens have been spotted every three days, so they can calculate the date when they should appear next and click it in the diary to get the next code.

The Control Room

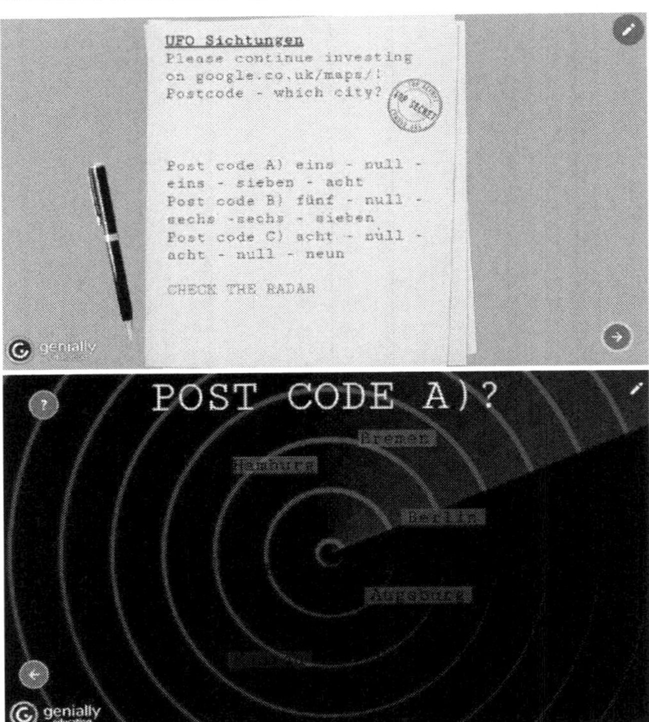

Players find a secret document in the control room telling them the postcodes of the last UFO sightings. Students need to translate the

German numbers and research which cities the postcodes belong to and find them on the radar. The rotating light here makes it more difficult to read the words as an extra challenge. The learning aim was to make students familiar with the look of German postcodes.

The Investigation Room

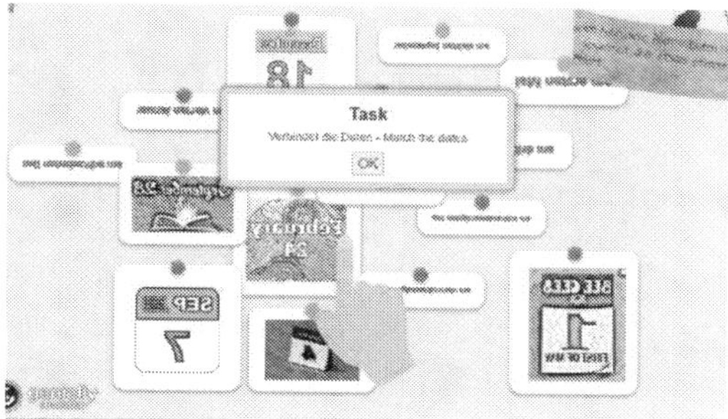

Image: www.learningapps.org

In the investigation room, students match up dates written in German and English in a LearningApps activity, but to make it more interesting, the English pictures are mirrored, and the German words are upside down.

The Map Room

There are two tasks in the map room. First, they have to look at five satellite maps and find a town that has a number in its name (they are all real towns). They can then use these numbers as the passcode on the computer.

Image: https://poly.google.com/creator/tours?dmr=0&pli=1

A Google VR tour is embedded in the computer: They can now look at one 360 degrees Google street view picture from each of the towns they have previously found on the maps and answer questions for each, e.g. How many blue umbrellas are there? What is the last number on the number plate? etc.

The Secret Lab

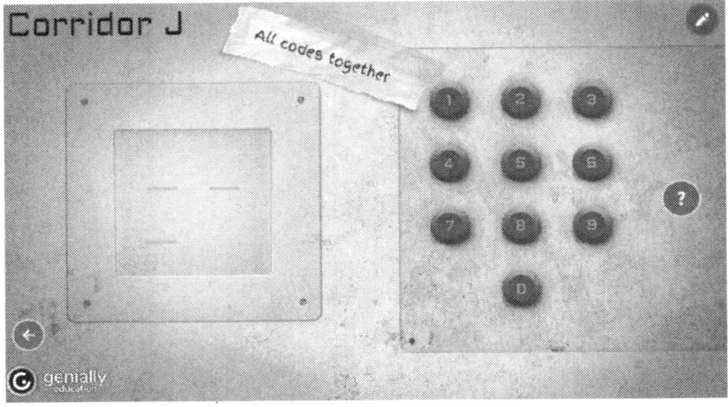

Finally, students arrive at a secret lab, and they need to add up all code numbers to gain entrance. In case the lock does not open, students can click the question mark, and a window with a Google form will pop up which they can use to check all the numbers they have collected. This way, they do not have to do all tasks again to find where their mistake is, and it saves the teacher from having to check all answers manually.

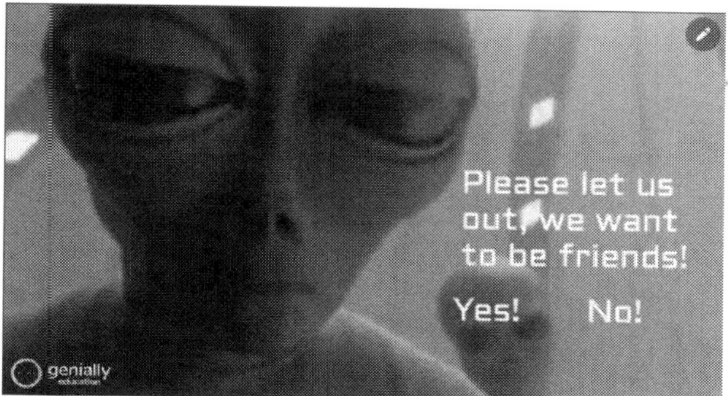

As the last task, students get a moral choice when they get into the lab: do they want to free the aliens or not? If the aliens are freed, you can see them flying off in their spaceship, otherwise, you see an animation of an alien attack (a GIF from the film "Independence Day"). In either case, players have the option to go back and decide differently. This choice at the end could be a starting point for an interesting discussion about alien life among the team members or the whole class during de-briefing.

REFERENCES

A document with all links and resources mentioned in this book can be found here:

http://bit.ly/morrisescape

Thanks to Brett Kuehner, http://www.thatguywiththepuzzles.com/, for sharing his list of resources on escape rooms with me.

Nicholson, Scott (2016) Ask Why: Creating a Better Player Experience Through Environmental Storytelling and Consistency in Escape Room Design
<http://scottnicholson.com/pubs/askwhy.pdf>

Elumir, Errol (2018) 2018 Escape Room Enthusiast Survey
<https://thecodex.ca/2018-escape-room-enthusiast-survey/>

Johnson, Holly (2018) Breaking into Breakout boxes, CreateSpace Independent Publishing Platform

Ross, Robert and Ross, Sarah (2020) Inescapable Learning: Unlock the power of educational escape rooms, Independently Published

Nicholson, Scott (due to be published 13 Feb. 2021) Unlocking the Potential of Puzzle-based Learning: Designing escape rooms and games for the classroom, SAGE Publications Ltd

Nicholson, Scott (2018) Creating engaging escape rooms for the classroom. Childhood Education 94(1). 44-49. http://scottnicholson.com/pubs/escapegamesclassroom.pdf

S'cape <https://scape.enepe.fr/>

Rosa, Luke *Students of History Lesson Resources* <https://www.studentsofhistory.com/>

Wiemker, Markus/ Elumir, Errol/ Clare, Adam (2015) Escape Room Games: "Can you transform an unpleasant situation into a pleasant one?" <https://thecodex.ca/wp-content/uploads/2016/08/00511Wiemker-et-al-Paper-Escape-Room-Games.pdf>

Cover image: Image by Clockendindk via pixabay.com <https://pixabay.com/illustrations/live-escape-game-live-escape-room-1155620/>

ABOUT THE AUTHOR

Image: Helen Myers

Julia Morris is a languages teacher in a secondary school in the South West of England. A native of Berlin, Germany, she has been working as a teacher in the UK for 13 years, teaching German and French. Julia is passionate about including technology and games in her lessons to increase student motivation and to make the lessons more fun to teach as well. Julia has been creating escape rooms and murder mysteries for her students for several years and her resources have been popular online with teachers in the USA, UK and many other countries. Julia has held training sessions on creating and running escape rooms in education for her school partnership and at the Technology in Language Teaching conferences organised by the Association of Language Learning London in 2019 and via webinar in 2020.

Printed in Great Britain
by Amazon